Tending the Soul

Learnings from a Lifetime of Spiritual Direction

Reverend Luke Dougherty, O.S.B.

RPI Publishing, Inc.

Published by RPI Publishing, Inc.
1725 Kresky Avenue
Centralia, WA 98531
(800) 873-8384
www.rpipublishing.com
ISBN 978-0-941405-58-4

Dougherty, Luke.
    Tending the soul : learnings from a lifetime of
    spiritual direction /
    Rev. Luke Dougherty. -- 1st ed. -- Centralia, WA :
    RPI Publishing, 2007.
        p. ; cm.
        ISBN: 978-0-941405-58-4
        Includes bibliographical references.
        1. Spiritual direction. 2. Spiritual life. I. Title.
BV5053 .D68 2007
253.5/3--dc22   0708

Written by Father Luke Dougherty
Developed by Barbara Milligan
Copy Edited by Kitty Kolody
Layout and Typeset by Roxanne Schick
Cover Art and Design by Madeline Wright
Printed in the United States of America
1st Edition & Print 08/2007
All scripture quotations, are taken from the Jerusalem Bible. Copyright 1968 by Random House, Inc. Used by permission. All rights reserved.

NOTICE: This book is designed to provide information regarding the subject matter covered. It is provided with the understanding that the publisher and author are not engaged in rendering individualized professional services.

· · · · · · · · · · · · · · ·

Preface

I remember well the first time I met Father Luke Dougherty, O.S.B. The occasion was not a surprising one: a forum on religious vocations being held at my parish. At the time, I was considering entering the seminary, and the one aspect of that evening that I still remember well, more than thirty years later, was this monk from the "Holy Hill" (then St. Charles Priory, now Prince of Peace Abbey), who so animatedly gave of himself in the ministries of vocation work, youth, faith formation, retreats, and above all, spiritual direction.

Little did I realize then how well I would come to know this holy man of God, and even more so, how well he would come to know me. I entered the seminary the following year and visited with Father Luke frequently during my years of priestly formation. Upon ordination, I asked him to be my spiritual director, and he directed me in the spiritual life from that time until his death.

During those twenty years I was also privileged to see Prince of Peace Abbey expand from its modest beginnings to what it is today. Rarely did I visit the monastery without seeing a building project in process, and this is an apt analogy for who Father Luke was to countless numbers of us who have benefited from his wise counsel. He built us up in the spiritual life, "walking the journey of faith" with us, as he was fond of saying, and helping us to mature in Christian virtue. He knew when to affirm us and be gentle, and when to challenge us and be direct.

This book is the fruit of a lifetime of study, reflection, and experience of spiritual direction, filtered through the unmistakable mind and heart of our dear Father Luke. Those of us who knew him well can sense his presence on every page. Indeed, a read-through of the book feels, almost hauntingly, like an encounter of spiritual direction with him.

Father Luke—he was our father, our mentor, our guide, and our friend. We miss him, but we are grateful to God for blessing us through him for so many years. May he now intercede for us before God's heavenly throne, until we all meet to be one in Christ Jesus and with each other for all eternity.

Requiem aeternam dona ei, Domine, et lux perpetua luceat ei. Requiescat in pace. (Eternal rest grant unto him, O Lord, and may perpetual light shine upon him. May he rest in peace.) Amen.

Most Rev. Salvatore Cordileone
Auxiliary Bishop of San Diego

Foreword

I met Father Luke Dougherty, O.S.B., in May 1962 at Prince of Peace Abbey. A student at San Diego State, I was interested in joining St. Charles Priory, as it was called then. Father Luke was a member of a small band of monks who had come from our founding abbey of St. Meinrad in Southern Indiana four years earlier to begin this new foundation in Southern California.

Father Luke's deep interest in people and their motives, goals, and relationships was apparent from the start. After a short time, he began graduate studies at Santa Clara University and was given the opportunity to work in a program for teenagers and young adults called Search for Christian Maturity. In my deacon year and the year following my ordination I worked closely with Father Luke in that program, by recruiting and training leaders and conducting intensive weekend retreats. Although he had always been a very capable spiritual director, this was where he began to develop on a larger scale. From the Search program Father Luke progressed to directing seminarians, and ultimately his work among so many members of the clergy has become legend. He was not only a sensitive spiritual director, but he also became a close friend to all with whom he worked.

This volume is a natural flow from the rich experiences and natural insights that graced Father Luke's entire life and helped so many to set spiritual goals and prayerfully discover ways of reaching those goals.

Rt. Rev. Charles Wright, O.S.B.
Abbot, Prince of Peace Abbey

Table of Contents

Introduction

The older we become, the more we wonder about the twists and turns of our own life's journey. My journey continues to be a step-by-step walk into the depth of God's love and God's gift to me. Among the valuable insights I have gained in this journey is an overwhelming sense of God's presence, power, and will at work in and through each person and event that became a part of every step of this journey. The ministry of spiritual direction and formative spirituality has been a constant and growing endeavor. Youth leadership and vocation work in the early years of my priestly ministry developed into some of the earliest efforts in dealing with seminary and priestly ministry, especially new forms of retreats. At the same time, I have been involved with retreats for religious sisters, brothers, and laity from all walks of life and professions. God indeed has blessed these efforts.

Today, as in every other period of history, people are asking, What is the meaning of my life? What is the direction of my life amidst all the advancements and advantages we enjoy? What direction are we really taking? People are seeking direction to begin to deal with those questions—to look at not only the things, people, and events going on around them, but more important, what is going on within them—what life is really about.

Spiritual direction is simple in its structures and methodology. The actual application and experience is where the real work needs to be done. For the last forty years I have provided spiritual direction, and I have been asked to share my experience—to illustrate some of the principal tools I have used and to show how they work. My vision of spiritual direction and the way I carried it out has been a personal response to the needs of individuals coming to me seeking guidance. This is not to say that my way is the only way. One would never say that the Benedictine monastic spirituality, for instance, is the only way to God—excluding the Ignatian, the Carmelite, the Franciscan, and the Dominican spirituality. Each is due praise and respect.

Each chapter title in this book represents a major tool I have used. Obviously, there are other tools that can be considered.

I have found that there is a constant dynamic between myself and those whom I direct. They gain insight by our work together, and I receive a great blessing from them. Many of the insights and wisdom in this book came as I walked the journey with them.

I hope that through this book you will feel invited to explore new ways of walking the spiritual journey with another.

Chapter 1

Companionship

A s the jet taxied down the runway, I eased back into my seat, looking forward to a quiet, restful flight. Because the flight would be long, I thought I might as well have a nodding acquaintance with the young man sitting next to me, so we greeted each other and shared some idle conversation. The more we talked, however, the more interested I became as he unfolded his story. He even knew some of the same people I knew, although he and I had just met.

He was a young executive striving to promote his position with a large company. When he learned that I was a priest on my way to a retreat assignment on the other side of the country, he began to tell me a little more about himself and his journey. He spoke of his family, his children, of whom he was obviously proud, and how he took every opportunity to be with them. I asked him, "How do you see your family values in relation to all the 'family values,' or lack thereof, that you see on television, in particular the television sitcom?" With this, the conversation went on and on. He was most proud of what he was able to do for his children. He also told me what he most appreciated about his family of origin. I mentioned to him that I found his thoughts, his comments, and his convictions to be important and refreshing. Since much of my work as a priest is in developing leadership, it was clear to me that this young man was a leader, unafraid to be himself.

Suddenly, over the speaker system, the pilot announced that we were about to begin the descent to our destination and that we would soon be on the ground. With that, the young man and I ended our conversation. What otherwise would have been a long and probably boring journey had become short and enjoyable.

My conversation with the young man is a good example of spiritual direction, because spiritual direction is about companionship on the spiritual journey of life. To walk this journey with another is an art—an art as old as Creation. It begins when one person seeks another person's advice about the journey of life. If we go to the book of Genesis in the Bible and proceed through the many books of the Bible, we will find example after example of this special kind of relationship in the spiritual journey.

Although many people participate in spiritual direction, it tends to be misunderstood. When a person asks me for spiritual direction, the first question I might think of is, "What is this person really asking for?" They might be seeking a number of different things. At first, they might be coming to me because they are in a crisis and need help in making an important decision. What they need in that case is crisis counseling, not spiritual direction. Or they might be looking for someone to take responsibility for their lives so that they do not have to bear the burden of that responsibility. That also is not spiritual direction. They might be looking for a way to solve a problem. But spiritual direction is not for the purpose of problem solving, either. Spiritual direction is simply the process of walking with another person on the journey of life.

As I look back over my experiences of spiritual direction with people from all walks of life, I find that I have learned, and am continuing to learn, to be a good listener. Listening is 95 percent of the work of a good spiritual director. However, in the context of spiritual direction, listening is not simply an intellectual process of hearing words. It means listening to the total person: Listening to the person's thoughts, obviously, but perhaps more important, listening to their feelings, their prejudices, their likes and dislikes, and getting to know the uniqueness of that person. As I begin, slowly, to understand the background and context of the journey that the person is sharing with me, I can enter into the all-important process of walking more closely with that person.

Having listened to the person, the next step is to reflect back to that person what I was hearing, just as I heard it, without any interpretation and without judgment. Saying, "It sounds like this is what you are thinking" or, "Here is what you seem to be feeling" gives the person an opportunity to see themselves and come to know themselves as they truly are. Spiritual direction has been compared to a mirror. We look into a mirror to see ourselves as we are. Otherwise we could be caught up in an illusion of who we are, and never know the reality of our true self, which is the basis for the conversion experience of the spiritual journey.

At this point in the exchange, I might share something from my own experience that seems appropriate to this person's situation. Finally, once the person has finished sharing whatever they want to share that day, I either affirm them in the direction they're taking or invite them to look at some other considerations. I might also invite them to rest in the present moment.

What I have just described is a general overview of the technique that I have found to be effective in walking the journey with another person. The ministry of spiritual direction is ever new, because each person who is seeking spiritual direction is a unique person and a new experience for me. I'm happy to say that spiritual direction has called me personally to grow in strength in this work.

The first requirement in the relationship between the spiritual director and the person seeking direction is an honesty that comes from deep within one's own self. Until we reach the level of honesty in which we can say things the way they are, we will not walk and grow together.

Some years ago the issue of honesty came up with a woman who was seeing me for direction. I found it necessary to tell her that it was important for both of us to be honest and that if she were unable to share with me what she was really thinking and feeling, I would be unable to help her. Immediately, she smiled and began to tell a much different, and true, story of her reason for seeking spiritual direction.

Another requirement of an effective spiritual direction relationship is openness—a level of trust that is built between the spiritual director and the person seeking direction. Trust takes time to develop. In the early meetings I am seeking to know the person just as much as that person is trying to know me. To find a base for trust is essential if any work is to be done.

You may have heard the story about the levels of trust that are evident in the level of conversation. There are five levels: weather, sports, politics, religion and self. The most none threatening, because it requires the least amount of trust, is weather. Moving into sports says a little more about the two people communicating; talking about politics says much more about them, as well as touches their feelings more deeply; then religion, which feels threatening to most people; and finally the self. We all tend to begin with level one, weather, and work up. The level of trust depends on the trust that we have established already. This trust depends on the respect of the two people in the direction process. As I direct someone, I must feel free to ask any questions that I feel are appropriate to help them understand their situation. If they are not willing to answer a question at the moment, I tell them we can come back to it later, and we move on. Sometimes a question may be too painful to pursue at that time.

In direction the focus of the communication is on the life of the individual seeking direction, not the director's life. Sometimes, people who come for spiritual direction ask the director personal questions, which takes the focus off them. In that case the director can respond gently, "We are here to talk about you and your journey."

The person seeking direction must feel, at all times, that their own thoughts and feelings are being respected. The growth that takes place through the process of spiritual direction is one of maturation. The person becomes more independent, not dependent on the director. For that reason, I as the director never make any decision for an individual or even recommend something that I believe would affect their independence in their decision-making process. I do not want them to feel that they cannot make their journey without me. God has called me into their lives for a certain time and purpose. Once that is accomplished, the relationship will change.

One final aspect that is important in the relationship of the director and the person seeking direction is a freedom to determine the nature and boundaries of the relationship, including the beginning and the end. Spiritual direction can last for one retreat, one year in the person's life, or quite a few years. The person seeking direction and the director have the freedom to discuss and agree where they meet, how frequently they meet, how long each session should last, and perhaps how long or how short a period the person seeking direction, spends in spiritual direction.

So how does a spiritual direction session proceed? Is there a pattern or format? When someone wants to begin seeing me for spiritual direction, I usually invite that person to come and spend some time, maybe a one-day retreat, maybe even a weekend, to become acquainted. Once we have become acquainted and have a general idea of where we are, the sessions are usually one hour, once every six weeks to two months, unless a situation in the person's life warrants more attention.

The session always begins with a prayer. Then I invite the individual seeking direction to bring up a point that they would like to discuss. For the first forty-five minutes I listen, ask questions, and draw a picture in my own mind of the issue that the individual is describing. We spend the next ten minutes talking about the issue and what particular action, if any, might be appropriate before the next meeting. Then the person decides on an action, and we conclude the session on the hour. So it's a one-hour session: thirty-five to forty-five minutes of input, a time of discussion, a resolution, and setting of the next appointment. This is the normal pattern I follow unless an extraordinary situation warrants to add twenty minutes more.

I have sometimes been asked, "Who would make the best spiritual director?" and, "What qualities should I look for in a director?" Spiritual direction, as I mentioned before, is walking with another person in their life's journey. A good spiritual director is one who offers something to reflect together on your own journey, because of their own faith and life experience. It can also be helpful to keep in mind your own personality type. I would look for a director who is different from me—not one who is going to agree with me on everything I say, but one who at times would challenge me, and at times would tell me things I don't want to hear but need to hear. It is important also to make your selection slowly and prayerfully. Choose someone with whom you can talk openly, someone with whom you can be honest and very open. This will allow you the freedom to be yourself in the relationship. You don't have to have a spiritual director immediately, like tomorrow. You might need to spend several months or a year asking God for that special person in your life who will be a light for you, a support to you in your own spiritual journey.

When a person comes to me for direction and is struggling with deep emotional issues, I try to bring this to the person's attention and encourage them to seek professional help, assuring them that if they do so, I would be happy to continue functioning as their spiritual director. In fact, I have found that it works more beneficially for the directee, if the spiritual director and the therapist can work together, with the permission of the directee. If the directee refuses to seek professional help and, perhaps without realizing it, tries to make me the therapist, I tell them that I cannot continue in spiritual direction with them.

One of the most important aspects of spiritual direction is confidentiality. It is just like the confidentiality of confessor and the person seeking reconciliation in the Sacrament of Reconciliation. Under no condition can the priest/confessor share any of the knowledge that he has come to know through this sacrament. This is vital, because on this confidentiality is built the bond of trust that draws the confessor and the penitent, as well as the spiritual director and the person seeking direction, together. If the confidence is ever broken, intentionally or not, the relationship is destroyed. I have always found it a good idea to thank the individuals for their confidence and their openness in our sessions, letting them know how much I appreciate their trust and their willingness to share so honestly.

Key Ideas: There are many factors that contribute to the establishment of healthy companionship in our lives; good listening, affirmation, honesty, trust, respect, etc. Companionship is an essential element in our spiritual journey. Reflect on your own interpersonal relationships. Which elements of companionship do you recognize as strengths, and which would you consider weaknesses in your relationships? Are you a good listener? If so, what makes you a good listener? If you struggle with this aspect of companionship what gets in your way? For example, what gets in your way of being a good listener to your wife or your children? Your friends and co-worker? How might you remove any obstacles to good listening?

Listening

The spiritual journey is one of listening to God speak to us. When we begin to realize that it is God who calls us, how are we to respond? Eli told the boy Samuel, "If someone calls, say, 'Speak, Yahweh, your servant is listening'" (1 Samuel 3:9). God speaks to us through Scripture, through tradition, through the significant people and events in our lives, and through our creation and redemption. And by creating and redeeming us, God has spoken to us directly. In each instance of God speaking to us, the important word is listening—and learning what it means to listen.

Sound can make an impact, but that is not the type of listening I am talking about. I'm talking about deep listening— listening to thoughts, to words, to feelings, to the heart and the instincts that God puts within us. When I considered entering the monastery, one of the attractions to monastic life for me was the silence of the monks. They seemed so peaceful and quiet going about their daily routine of prayer and work. After I entered the monastery, much to my surprise, this very silence became the first obstacle I needed to overcome. Monastery life plunged me into a life of silence in which all the normal distractions were taken away: No newspapers, no television, no radio, very few magazines, maybe the sports page once a week, but certainly no Sunday comics. Abruptly, I realized I had stepped into another world. As time went by, the silence became more comfortable for me. It wasn't until a year and a half later, when I took my first vows, that I realized how much I had changed—how much had happened and how much I had entered into the silence that had made it possible for me, for the first time in my life, to begin to listen.

There is a call within each one of us to come together, to be one—to be the gift of God that we are, God having created us, gifted us, and redeemed us—and to hear what God would have us do to accomplish his will in our lives. This is a sure and true way to happiness on the road to the God toward whom we travel throughout our lives in our spiritual journey.

The development of the spirituality of prayer, in recent times, has begun with the listening experience, or what we call a desert experience, when everything seems shut down. We live in a noisy world today. Science and technology have filled our lives and our minds with images and a myriad of sounds. We have to go against the culture to find that life-giving silence so that we can hear God in the depths of our hearts and at the center of our true selves. People today are seeking that silence in which they can find their true selves and the God within. This is where we can come to know God and to know his will. This is, as I said earlier, the destination of the spiritual journey—to know God the Father, Jesus Christ the Son, and the great gift of the Holy Spirit; and in Jesus, to know and to love each other. This is the course of our journey in this world.

How do we start listening to God? Listening is easier if we've been talking to God. Some years ago I saw a film of a man with a microphone interviewing people on a busy street. The man asked, "When was the last time you talked to God?" It was interesting to see the expressions on everyone's face and to hear their answers: "What?" "You've got to be kidding!" "Do you think I'm crazy?" "You must be a fanatic!" When someone comes to me for direction, I sometimes suggest that they write a letter to God. In this letter, they can tell God who he is for them; where God is in their lives at this moment; what is mysterious about his presence; what they would like most to receive from God; and what kind of relationship they want to have with God. I ask the person to write the letter in a quiet place, in prayer, and with deep reflection—reflecting their deepest, most intimate feelings, as well as their thoughts.

Once the individual has written this letter to God, we can begin our exercise of listening. I invite them to sit down and listen carefully as I, with their permission, read the letter out loud. I ask them to do a reverse role-play for the moment, in which I am the person seeking direction, and they are the director. Then they can more easily listen and truly hear what I am saying. As they hear their own words, they begin to truly hear what they are saying, because to write is to objectify our thoughts, our feelings, and our instincts, which are otherwise buried deep within us. For this reason, one of the most effective tools in spiritual direction is the spiritual journal, in which the individual makes daily entries or whenever their spirit moves them. Then they bring the journal to the direction session and continue to reflect on what they have said.

What is happening here is that the person is beginning to recognize their inner journey. I use the term inner journey to distinguish it from the outer journey. People and events on the surface of life happen to us as we journey in a chronological fashion, but at the same time there is a journey going on within us, very deeply within our soul—our spiritual journey. It is by listening to this journey that we begin to answer the deeper questions of our lives: "Who am I?" "What am I?" "Where am I going?"

At the heart of this inner journey is the true self, and at the heart of the true self is God. Here is where we find God, his will, his word, and his ways. As we listen carefully, our lives are transformed from the inside, which changes our outer journey as well as our inner journey. I believe that most of us in our noisy, busy world don't take the time or make the space to truly listen, because listening is an art that requires practicing necessary skills.

Listening is the key to many situations. A few years ago, a friend of mine—let's call him Ed Michaels—refused to face the truth that his mother was dying of leukemia. Ed was unable to listen to his dying mother when she wanted to talk about the practical arrangements, when she wanted to talk about her life, when she wanted to express her love. Ed insisted on making plans for her that she did not want. He joked, he teased her, and he brought her presents. He did everything but listen to her and really talk with her. Consequently, his mother's anger, confusion, and suffering increased. The turning point for him came when a reporter working with Ed, who was a newspaper editor, came to visit Ed's mother at a time that both the doctor and Ed were there. When the reporter asked the doctor, who was known for his work with dying patients, to speak to Mrs. Michaels, the doctor responded, "I won't speak to her, but I will listen to her."

Ed was afraid to listen. When he did begin to listen, he was hurt and confused and afraid, but he was also warm, close, and alive. He was finally able to help his mother as she was dying. When we refuse to listen, we cut ourselves off from ourselves and from others.

There are many situations when we refuse to listen. "Don't tell me—I don't want to know" is a common escape. Pain can be a friend, a signal to go to the doctor or dentist, but we may refuse to acknowledge it and pretend we don't notice it nagging us. The doctor advises us to lose weight, to get more exercise, or to cut down on drinking or smoking, but we may ignore the doctor's advice. The car makes funny noises, but we pretend that the warning signals are not there. It's easy to do the same thing in our relationships, not to listen to others. When a person suddenly begins to act strangely, often it's their way of saying, "I need more love and attention," or "I don't know how to handle my situation." It is simply easier to ignore the behavior than to listen for the message.

Listening to God's Word

At times it may be difficult to listen to the Word of God and apply it in our own lives, especially when we are presented with a chance for some easy, self-serving pleasure. How do we respond to this in a Gospel manner? Strangely enough, it is even harder to hear encouraging words—to hear that the news is good, that God is loving and provident, that deep-down things are in his care despite turmoil on the surface.

The Word of God, the Holy Scripture, cries out to us. The cry is that the news is good, that God does care, that God listens to us, and that there is a power to enable us to hear the Word of God, then the words of those around us, and finally, our own inner words. In St. Mark's story of Jesus curing the deaf man (Mark 7: 31-37), the man was immediately able to hear and to speak clearly after Jesus touched the man's ears, anointed them, and commanded his ears to be open.

The cure of our deafness could be just as swift, but usually it is a lifelong process. The process begins at our baptism and continues throughout our lives. We are all more or less deaf, and we need to stand before Christ, as the man in the Gospel story did, and ask Jesus to lay his healing hands on us. Each of us is deaf in our own way, and we half know what it is we are failing to hear. Perhaps we are failing to heed some demands in our life—demands for honesty, justice, chastity, or truth. Hearing the demands is difficult. Yet listening and responding is never as terrifying as we fear. Perhaps we are deaf to the needs, hurts, and wants of those around us. It's easy to turn a deaf ear to someone who is asking for our concern and our help. All that is needed sometimes is a few minutes of listening. Maybe we prefer to cling to our feelings of hurt and sorrow and find it difficult to listen to the good news that we can trust in God. The ironic part is that our hurt and sorrow often are cured by forgetting about ourselves and listening to the cries of others. By listening to others, we are cured by the action of the Holy Spirit.

Silence

If we are going to listen, silence is necessary. This silence is not just an absence of external noise and distractions, but that deep interior silence that lets the mind, and especially the heart, rest in the Lord. This is an absolute necessity if we are to experience any growth and depth in our prayer life or in our walk with God. Today many are seeking solitude and silence away from all the noise and distraction that are so much a part of our daily lives. Jesus, in speaking to the scribes and Pharisees gives us some words to ponder: "You will listen and listen again, but not understand, see and see again, but not perceive" (Matthew 13:10-17). If we see and hear, our hearts will then be converted. So let us see, then, the place in our spiritual journey, and the definite place to do the work of walking the spiritual journey, but see it with prayerfulness in the silence that would lead us ever deeper into the reality of God, of ourselves, and of each other.

Key Ideas: To know God, to know his will, to know our true self, we must enter into our inner journey. Silence is the pathway to this inner spiritual world. By creating silence we can listen to what God is saying to us, we can come to know our true self, and accomplish God's will in our life. Consider your own life at this moment, what are the "distractions" that inhibit you from becoming silent? What "noises" prevent you from listening to the quiet voice of God speaking to your inner soul?

The Story

When someone is seeking a spiritual director, it is usually because of a grace that is arising from within. However, sometimes the person might think: "When I find the right spiritual director, my work will be over. The director will tell me God's will for me. My present confusion will dissolve in a session or two." The truth of the matter is that I will invite them to begin to reflect prayerfully on their journey and their life as they understand it now. Put simply, I will ask them to write and to reflect on their own unique story.

God has been speaking to each of us from the moment we were conceived in our mother's womb. God has spoken through the people and events in our lives. It is important to recall the people and events that are significant in our lives, because they have helped make each of us who we are today. Also, as we look to the future, we know that this wonderful work God is doing continues from where it started, from God, and leads back to God, through the people and events that fill our lives. This pattern is clearly exemplified in the autobiography of Thomas Merton, *The Seven Story Mountain*[1].

One way that we can pull together the people and events of our lives and prepare to meditate prayerfully on our unique story is to create a timeline. An example of the timeline is included at the end of this chapter.

Here's how I suggest creating it. First, take a piece of paper, $8^{1}/2$ x 11 inches, and turn it sideways. Next, use a ruler to draw a horizontal line from side to side. Write the year of your birth on the left side, and write the present year on the right side.

List on the sheet of paper all the people you can remember who have positively or negatively influenced your life. Include parents, siblings, relatives, coaches, movie stars, etc.

Next, create a list of events that have positively or negatively affected you deeply, perhaps even changed the course of your life or formed your life in some way. For example, when I was in the second grade I received a certificate for good penmanship. I was proud of it, so it was a positive experience. Among the negative experiences in my earliest years, I can remember neighbors who kept a ferocious bulldog in a pen. Whenever I walked past that house, the dog charged toward the fence. The threatening sounds of the barking and growling filled me with the fear that if somehow that dog were to get loose, he would attack me in a harmful way. To this day, whenever I have a ferocious encounter with a dog, I have those same negative feelings.

When the list of people and events is complete, record the events chronologically along the timeline, beginning with your birth and working through your childhood and teenage years, from young adulthood to adulthood, and if applicable, to your mature years and to a second-or third-career phase of your life. Inserting all these things along this line enables you to see many of your significant moments at a glance. Then draw a line that connects these influences and events. If it was a positive influence or event, insert the information above the timeline; if it was a negative influence or event, insert the information below the timeline. Draw a line connecting the people and events. The resulting line will demonstrate a pattern of your journey. Each of us has a unique pattern of behavior, one that has been with us and continues to grow with us and normally does not vary unless there is a major change in our values and our priorities. We will talk about these later.

The timeline becomes a tool to help you take the next step, that is, slowly and prayerfully to write the story of your life as you can remember it, a story that is your own. But most important, you will find that there are definite messages about your life, your journey, about God, about those whom God has called to journey with you, and about the destination of that journey.

Now create a second timeline. Call it Timeline II. This time the focus is different, although the method is the same. In this timeline you will record your own unique story of your relationship with God. Make a timeline of your faith journey, listing the people and events that had a positive or negative effect on your relationship with God. As you look at this timeline prayerfully, you'll see certain patterns in your story that are extremely important for the journey ahead.

In asking you for your own unique story, I realize I am asking you to do something that you may at first find challenging. To stop and reflect might not be easy, but as you do it, you will begin to grow in your awareness of the story, how unique it is, and how God has been, is now, and will continue to be, at work in your life. I want to emphasize that this story is written for you. You will share it with your spiritual director only if you feel comfortable doing so. It will give you and your spiritual director a basis upon which your faith journey will continue to deepen. Once you write your story, it is something that I hope you will cherish. You can take it out and read it again many times. It can become a source of prayer and of new insight. It can make you aware of how much God loves you and how present he is to you. It can become something that significantly affects your prayer life and your relationship with God.

I like to draw out, from my own story, three points that constantly change and that have been a source of much reflection. I try to list the highest point, the lowest point, and the most mysterious point in my life to date. I then reflect on why I made certain choices at those times in my life. By recording those choices, I can look back later and see how I might have changed, and see how the hand of God is in control of my journey.

I also like to think of one significant person in my life and write about why I appreciate that person, how that person entered my life, how my life was changed, and how that person continues to be present today. Again, this is a gift of God.

Finally, as I reflect upon the story, I like to choose the most powerful event in my faith journey that changed my life. I like to meditate on the event, and to reflect on how it continues to have an effect me.

Key Ideas: Take the time to record your "story." The process of reflection on whom you have been, who you are, and who you may become, is not a momentary experience, but an endeavor over time. Our Father writes the pages of your "story." If you do not listen to the "story" being told by God on the canvas of your life, then you will neither experience accomplishment nor completeness. The oneness that God invites you to create with him is found in your own unique "story." God has been speaking to you all of your life through individuals and events. Share in the authorship of your "story" and share it with your Spiritual Director or with another whom you trust.

1. Thomas Merton *The Seven Storey Mountain*
(New York: Harcourt Brace, 1948).

Timeline I – *Example*
My Life Journey

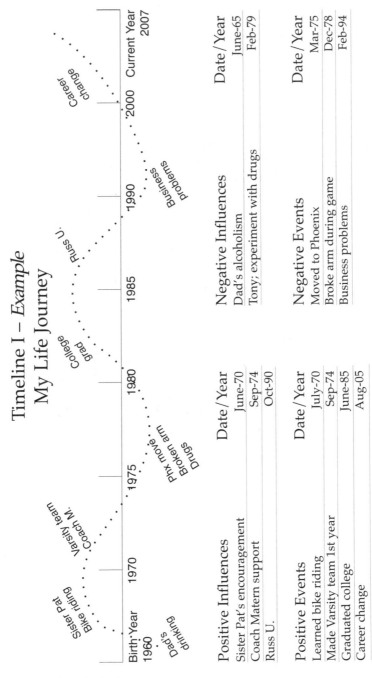

	Date/Year
Positive Influences	
Sister Pat's encouragement	June-70
Coach Matern support	Sep-74
Russ U.	Oct-90

	Date/Year
Positive Events	
Learned bike riding	July-70
Made Varsity team 1st year	Sep-74
Graduated college	June-85
Career change	Aug-05

	Date/Year
Negative Influences	
Dad's alcoholism	June-65
Tony; experiment with drugs	Feb-79

	Date/Year
Negative Events	
Moved to Phoenix	Mar-75
Broke arm during game	Dec-78
Business problems	Feb-94

Timeline II – *Example*
My Faith Journey

Pastor John
Baptism

Prof. Shipley

After Call

New Agers
New Age

Cursillo

Father Bill
RCIA

Business struggle

Father Sharbel

Birth Year
1960
1970
1975
1980
1985
1990
2000
Current Year
2007

Positive Influences	Date/Year
Pastor John	June-65
Prof. Shipley	Sep-79
Father Bill	Sep-94
Father Sharbel	Mar-04

Positive Events	Date/Year
Baptism	Dec-60
Cursillo	Oct-87
RCIA	Sep-94

Negative Influences	Date/Year
Ann and Jack M.	June-81
New Age groups	Apr-82
Business struggles	Feb-92

Negative Events	Date/Year
Coerced to do altar call	Dec-72

Conversion

G od calls each of us uniquely to be ourselves and then to carry out a particular work, his work, in this world. As we identify our unique story and journey we come to realize who we are and what we are called to do. The process of coming to know who we are in God, and what his plan is for us, is called conversion. Our lives are a lifelong conversion experience.

To be converted is to change, and to change is to grow. To grow, we need to change. In fact, we need to change often as we grow because we are converted in the journey of a lifetime. The change in growth is reflected in the change of our values and priorities over a period of time.

Some years ago I attended a conference for religious educators in which Dr. Sidney Simon told us that we are our values and that as we come to know our values, we come to know ourselves. He defined a value as that which, given the time and freedom, we would spend our time and our energy developing. He asked us to list, in the middle of a sheet of paper, our five top values at this time in our lives, in order of priority, keeping in mind not what we believe our values should be, but how we use our time in any given twenty-four hours. For example, if we spend much time on the golf course, or shopping, that is a value. If we spend little or no time in prayer, that is not a value no matter what we might want to say. Then we were to move to the left side of our paper and list our five values as we can remember them seven years ago. Finally, on the right side of the paper, we listed our values as we might envision them to be seven years into the future. As we looked at our three columns, we readily noticed the changes. Remember that change is growth, and growth is change.

I invite you to do this exercise and see where the changes have occurred in your own life. The change will come particularly in the priority of your values. Some things that were very important to you seven years ago, maybe even top priority, today might not even be on your current list of five. As you look forward to seven years from now, there are things that today you hold dear and spend an enormous amount of time and energy doing but will not be at the top of your list, or may have slipped to third or fourth on your list, or may not even be there at all.

This little exercise can give you an opportunity to begin to realize, perhaps more than you ever have before, that we do change—that what is here today was not here yesterday and will not be here tomorrow. What is here today is today.

In the spiritual life, we live in the present moment. Spirituality is reality. Your story is a way of entering into the reality, not only in the present moment with the current people and events in your life, but as a way of looking back to understand your background and where you came from. It also gives you precious insight into the direction your journey might be leading you. It might even point out to you where your next conversion will be.

I would now invite you to take up your Holy Scripture and identify this conversion experience. The beginning of a response to the unique call from God to "come and follow me" is the conversion experience reflected in the changes in our values and priorities. So, for example, we have the values of this world, the here and the now and the superficial, against the Christian values—the values of the hereafter, the supernatural. Under the values of this world we have, for example, sexuality in which a person becomes an object, while Jesus tells us, "Love one another as I have loved you." (John 15:12). Take the person, completely, as a person truly loved and cherished by God. In worldly values we find escapism in many forms, especially in pleasure. The Christian value is to follow Jesus, who said that unless we deny ourselves daily and take up our cross and follow him, we are not worthy of him. We are called not to escape the pain of life, but to embrace it and through that very pain to grow in love in our relationship to God and to each other.

The worldly value is power over other people; the more we can manipulate people to our advantage, have them serve us, the better—I'm number one. In the Christian value, Jesus says, "The Son of Man came not to be served but to serve" (Matthew 20:28). Do we follow his example in our daily journey?

Another worldly value is that money equals power. The Christian value, however, is to follow Jesus' words: "Sell all that you own…; then come, follow me" (Luke 18:22).

There's the worldly value of self-gratification: Everything is for me. Everything starts and ends with me. Jesus tells us the Christian value: "Unless a wheat grain falls on the ground and dies, it remains only a single grain; but if it dies, it yields a rich harvest" (John 12:24).

Looking at the Scripture, and at our lived experience, we can see that the values of the world around us proclaimed day after day, particularly in the media, are the values of the here and now. Over and against those values, the conversion experience for us is to change and to grow, to change from the values of this world, to leave them behind, and to embrace Christian values, to embrace Christ.

Turn with me to the letter to the Philippians, in which St. Paul summarizes his life before and after conversion. He describes his own change from his values as a leader in his own religion, among the Jewish leaders—

the scribes, Pharisees, and teachers—to his new values as a follower of Christ. St. Paul says, "I look on everything as so much rubbish if only I can have Christ and be given a place in him. . . . All I want is to know Christ and the power of his resurrection..."(Philippians 3: 8-10). This example of conversion stands before us and calls us to look at it again and again; to look at our lives—where we are in the conversion process—to be in close touch with our values and priorities. How do we spend our time? What does that say about us? We are our values.

The question of values and priorities becomes especially important when we consider vocational choices. We ask ourselves, "What does God want me to do?" God's will is manifested in our thoughts, our desires, and our aspirations. We might even think that we choose God. God is one of our options—I want to become a part of God's team and grow as part of God's plan. Yet, the more we pray and reflect, and look at all the human criteria for making vocational career choices, we find that such things as job description, likes and dislikes, and many other very human considerations all drop away and our one question becomes, "What is God calling me to do?" No way do I choose God, or be so rash as to think that I chose God. God does the choosing. In faith and humility, in getting in touch with our own story, our journey to date, as well as our own talents, we find the will of God, God's plan for us, our unique call in a clear and strong way. Never let us forget, though, that the mystery of our call from God is a call to be one with Christ. As St. Paul tells us in his Letter to the Philippians, we are all called to be part of the mystery of Christ. The introduction to the letter of the Ephesians is also well worth pondering. God's will, God's design for each of us, is eternal and specific. God loves each of us and calls us to respond as only we can respond (see Ephesians 1:3-19).

When we look at our true values and where we are in our journey, these are two things that a spiritual director can help us with and signify that we are well into seeking God's will. I came face-to-face with needing to look at my own values when I was chosen to be one of the founding members for a new monastery in California. I was in a large community with a well established monastic discipline and with my every need taken care of. But the day came when we left the archabbey for California and moved into a world that was strictly unknown to us, and that was at first a traumatic experience for me. When we arrived, instead of having a large community, there were only six of us. Things that we took for granted in a well established monastery weren't there. We had to establish them ourselves. This brought about a lot of change and growth in all of us, and it changed my life forever. The values and priorities were upside down, and the most important consideration of all was that we could only manage to be comfortable.

Among the values when we began our foundation were: prayer, community, various forms of ministry, and maybe some form of recreation. These values were changed in the order of priorities by the situation of the moment and were changing day by day. I am happy to say that as we look back to those first days, the values that we sacrificed for remained with us as we grew and became a better-known community. The struggles we went through and the changes we had to make, we can now look back on as cherished memories. It has been gratifying that we brought with us a formation in our values from the founding monastery and that those values have become more and more a part of our community today as we have stabilized and grown.

The selection of St. Paul's letter to the Philippians has been an excellent guide for me throughout my life This enabled me to keep in touch with my own ongoing experience of conversion. The conversion experience can be a life-giving pattern that repeats itself again and again as we continue to grow into Christ and follow his will.

Key Ideas: In knowing your "story," you come to know Our Father and His will for us. This kind of knowing creates direction, meaning, and purpose in your journey. In today's world, knowing your true self seems a remote priority. You may strive to be like others, accepted by others, to be something other than who you are. If your values reflect who you are, then to live as your true self means you are living out your true values. Following the world's values, the story it wishes you to live, can only lead to unhappiness. What values can be found in your life's journey, in your "story." Spend time reflecting, journaling your unique story. You will discover who God is, what He has in store for you, and who God created you to be. This is the gift of conversion.

Gifts

In the course of history societies and nations have always found ways to honor gifted people. We have the Nobel Peace Prize; in the entertainment industry, we have the Oscars; for literature, we have the Pulitzer Prize. We could go on with a long list of ways that gifted people are recognized and put before us as role models. The reward of this recognition is fame, money, honor—all those things that the world values so highly. In fact, this recognition can go so far that the individuals who accept these honors are put to the test of how they handle it. We have the witness of Mother Theresa of Calcutta, who was recognized by the world with many awards for her compassion in her work with the poor. Each time she was rewarded, she immediately passed her gifts on to the poor and needy. This made her witness even more powerful and effective.

While some gifted people are recognized, many more gifted people are not recognized, and they might be even more gifted than some who are recognized. God gives each of us special gifts that are unique to us individually.

As you pray over and try to respond to the questions this book asks you to consider, remember that there are no right or wrong answers. What I suggest you look for in this prayerful reflection is the response that tells you where you are at this moment, the response that gives you a better awareness of the values and priorities in your life. There is no need to escape to the future—just wait until then, and I'll be this perfect person. Nor is there any point in dwelling on the mistakes of the past, because we know that we all are sinners, that we are broken. We walk the journey of life. We make mistakes and life goes on.

Jesus, in calling each of us to be one with him, to be converted, to embrace him and the Good News he brought to change our lives and the lives of those around us, is not asking us to change our personality so that we become a perfect person, completely gifted with no weaknesses. Instead, he calls each of us to accept ourselves as we are, to deal with what is there. That means living in the present moment. That is the only important thing to keep in mind because that is the only thing we can deal with effectively. It's important to know ourselves and where we are, but also to learn what it means to grow. That is the real issue that we want to look at now.

Time is an important factor in this process of learning about ourselves and how we respond constructively to what we see at any given time in our lives. God means us to be intellectually and emotionally comfortable with ourselves. When I say "comfortable" I do not mean complacent. I do mean comfortable in that we know ourselves and accept ourselves.

Let's go back to the Holy Scripture and look at the call of Jeremiah (Jeremiah 1:1-10). When the Lord called Jeremiah to be a prophet, Jeremiah looked for an excuse: "Ah, Lord Yahweh; look, I do not know how to speak: I am a child!" Jeremiah had a poor self-image. He felt that surely the Lord would be calling someone else, not him. But God had a purpose for choosing Jeremiah. God also has a purpose in calling each of us to our work here in this life. God calls us and takes us as we are, just as he did with Jeremiah.

In the history of spirituality, we have the wonderful examples of those who have gone before us, saintly people, particularly priests and religious. They become for us models that are sometimes unreal. When I entered the religious life many years ago, as often happens when people enter the seminary or the convent, I came to a building with a large entrance. At the entrance stood a statue of a model priest. As I entered into the house of formation, I expected that I would come out looking just like that statue. I would be the model religious or priest. However, my expectation, I later found out, was unreal.

Models exist to inspire us and to give us a goal to strive toward. The model will always be there as a model. Each of us will be the person that we are because God called us to be who we are and where we are at any given moment. He works in us just as we are. Jesus said, "If you will be perfect, come follow me. He did not say, "Be perfect and then come follow me." Here I am using the word perfection in the sense of complete. This means fully realizing our God-given potential, using our gifts to the fullest, to the glory of God, to the service of others, and to meet our own needs.

God is going to work in you and through you, as you are. This is the mystery of the call we have received from God. We might even say that it is too good to be true, and in a sense it is. Nevertheless, it is true. You might say, "I don't have that kind of potential." But who knows? You could be another Jeremiah. Or you might say, "Although I can do a few things well and I get satisfaction from them, for the most part I'm dissatisfied with myself." When you reach this point, it is time for you to discover the person that you are. This is no easy task. Look in the Gospels at the apostles and other friends of Jesus, such as Martha and Mary. Consider the difference between Peter, the prince of the apostles, and John, the beloved disciple; Mary, the contemplative, and Martha, the busy homemaker. We know what Jesus said to his chosen when they were in the boat on the Sea of Galilee and on other occasions. He reprimanded them for their lack of faith. When Jesus predicted his passion, Peter said, "This must not happen to you." Jesus responded, "Get behind me, Satan!" (Matthew 16:22-23). The apostles did not hide their real selves; as Peter said when Jesus miraculously filled their fishing nets with fish, "Leave me, Lord; I am a sinful man" (Luke 5:8).

Here is an exercise that proved helpful to me as I considered my gifts. I took a sheet of paper, 8^1/2 x 11 inches, and made a list of my gifts and weaknesses—to the left, my gifts, and on the right, my weaknesses. When I began to list my gifts, immediately I thought, "Indeed, I find this very difficult. I am too humble to do that."

Never let us forget that humility is truth. The truth is that our gifts are God's gifts entrusted to us. As we recognize our gifts, given to us by God, we honor him by using our gifts and giving God the credit for them. As gifts from God, they need to be recognized and used.

I continued to list my gifts, the things I do well, and I was able to accept them as gifts. Then, on the other side of the page, I listed my weaknesses, bearing in mind that they should not be identified in a negative way. Negativism is not productive. The more negative we are about ourselves, the more we become bogged down in our negative thoughts and feelings. Our weaknesses simply indicate to us the areas where we need to grow and to change. For that reason, they can be the most exciting areas in our spiritual lives.

After I listed my weaknesses, I totaled the number of entries in each column and found that the number of gifts far outweighed the number of weaknesses. Among my gifts are the great gifts of God's love and forgiveness. These are real gifts that each of us receives again and again in our lives. God's gifts offset the weaknesses so much that we learn to accentuate the positive. If I become excited about my giftedness, how good God has been to me, what capabilities God has given me, and I use them generously and lovingly, I will find out that by accentuating the positive, the negative will simply disappear from lack of attention. The more I take my attention away from being negative and instead spend my time and energy in being positive, I find that I move and grow in the giftedness in which God has called me uniquely.

There is another thought about weakness to keep in mind. God works through our weaknesses. As St. Paul says, "I glory in my weaknesses, that the power of Christ may be made manifest in me." Where we are broken, where we are weak, there exactly is where we find God's presence and God's power operating in our lives.

Knowing yourself and accepting yourself are two distinct phases in our growth. I may know myself and not like what I see. Then I will opt for some kind of a mask, the one that I think others want me to wear. This mask pleases others and makes me popular with them. It is normal to have defenses, or masks, when we are not sure of ourselves. As we grow in life, we all take off masks when we become sure of who we really are. We come to know that God loves us as we are and has gifted us to take a unique place in his plan. In the sight of God, we do not have to prove ourselves to be loved. God accepts us just as we are and loves us as we are. God loves us unconditionally and forgives unconditionally. It is a rule that my self-worth is not bound up in what I can or cannot do to prove myself. It is important that as we look at our gifts and weaknesses, we learn to say to ourselves, "Love me. Take me as I am, because I am lovable."

It is important to share your list of gifts and weaknesses with a spiritual friend, perhaps your spiritual mentor or spiritual director, to tell that person where you are. No one knows us better than the people around us. The matter of spiritual friendships is something we will take up later in this book, but suffice it to say here, that in the matter of coming to know ourselves, to have someone to reflect back to us who we really are, what we really think, and what we really feel. The more we come to know ourselves and appreciate ourselves as we are, the more we are able to turn to God in a prayer of thanksgiving for his goodness, his love, his gifts, and the weaknesses in us that draw us closer to him, realizing that everything comes from God and is meant to lead us back to God. Our gifts do this, certainly, but just as well, our weaknesses, because this is the will of God. Both our gifts and our weaknesses become our way of coming back home to him, our loving and compassionate Father, who loves us unconditionally and accepts us just as we are.

Key Ideas: As we discover who we are, in silence, listening, we unveil the truth of who we are in Christ. We not only discover our true self, but we come to know how God, Our Father, is uniquely reflected in us. The purpose of our life is held within the "who we are" of our story. In deepening this knowing of self we must acknowledge and accept our strengths and weaknesses. Consider your gifts, your talents and abilities. Identify your weaknesses. Spend time reflecting on the "masks" that you have created in order to conceal certain aspects of yourself. What "masks" do you wear? What elements of your true self do they cover-up? What are the consequences of these "masks" in your relationship with God, with others, and with yourself?

Prayer

When I was heavily involved in vocation discernment work for about twenty years, particularly vocations to the priesthood and religious life, I received thousands of brochures from other dioceses and religious orders for men and women throughout the country. In all the brochures, prayer was mentioned as something that was understood, or taken for granted. In the brochures that included pictures, there might be a picture of a sister or father out where the action was, either the father in the pulpit expounding the Word of God with a heavenly look on his face, or a sister in the perfect classroom, with each student giving rapt attention as she shared her gift for imparting knowledge. But at least one picture in the brochure would show the priest or sister at prayer with an open book, be it the Liturgy of the Hours or the Word of God itself, a crucifix on the wall, and again, a heavenly glow around the person in prayer.

Our first response to the call of Christ to "come and follow me" is not work, but prayer. Look at Mark's Gospel: Jesus "went up into the hills and summoned those he wanted. So they came to him and he appointed twelve; they were to be his companions and to be sent out to preach, with power to cast out devils" (Mark 3:13-15). Jesus' call is to be his companion, which means to develop a relationship with him. I find that relationship is the best word for defining and understanding the all-important significance of prayer.

As I look back on my own experience of prayer, I go back to high school seminary days. Every day during the school year, after classes in the afternoon and recreation, I came in from the football field or the basketball court to the study hall, and for half an hour before dinner there was a time of spiritual reading. As one might imagine, in those twelve years of preparation for ordination, many books on prayer were part of that spiritual reading. I read about all the methods of prayer—those of St. Ignatius, St. Benedict, St. Francis, St. John of the Cross, St. Theresa of Avila. All of them inspired me, and I deeply admire all the great spiritual founders. However, their methods of prayer didn't relate to me where I was in my own relationship with God.

Many years later I came across a book by Father Edward Farrell titled *Prayer Is a Hunger*[1]. Reading that book was a great grace to me, because in his first chapter he says that prayer is not a thing to do, but it is a relationship. That doesn't mean that the many hours and days I had spent in prayer up to that time were not prayer. I was indeed in relationship to God—to Jesus, the Father, and the Spirit. But I finally realized that prayer is a hunger. Therefore, to understand prayer, I had to look at my relationship with God at its deepest level.

I want to distinguish between several kinds of prayer. There is communal prayer, the Liturgy of the Hours, when we pray together. The summit, the greatest expression of this community prayer, is the Eucharist. This is the perfect prayer, the prayer of Jesus. We become one with him, and in him we become one with each other. The basis of that union is personal prayer—time spent together with the Lord in relationship. From that relationship flows a richness in our community prayer and ultimately a deeper celebration of the great mystery of love, of my relationship to Christ and to others. We acknowledge this mystery each time we celebrate the Holy Eucharist.

So how does one begin to appreciate prayer as relationship? For me, the best way is to think of the person in my life's journey whom I consider to be a best friend. How did that relationship happen? Did it just happen? Did I meet this person one day and immediately we were best friends? I think not. Rather, friendship is a process. True and lasting friendships include three important elements: presence, sharing, and self-sacrifice. This is especially true in building a friendship with God through prayer.

Let's look at the first element, presence. To know someone and to be present to that person are not the same thing. To be and to do are separate realities. If I am going to pray to God, who is my friend, I must first be present. Again, I ask, "How did my friend become my best friend?" Well, the first thing is that we have to meet each other. Let's say I have a friend named Mark. Perhaps I first heard about Mark from his friends, and he might have heard of me. He and I admire and respect each other. Let's say that Mark writes me a letter, and I happily respond. Let's say further that this correspondence goes on for some time until, finally, I invite Mark to come to the monastery to see me so that I have a chance to meet him—and he comes. Until this point, I don't really know Mark. I might surmise from his voice that he is a middle-aged man, intelligent and friendly. Nor does Mark know who this Father Luke is, this monk at the monastery. Like many people do, perhaps he thinks of monks as being a bit stocky, bald-headed, always smiling— you know, the Friar Tuck type. Mark comes to the monastery, and all of a sudden there I am. He sees me. I see him. At that moment, being present to each other is the most important thing in our relationship.

I say to Mark, "Welcome to the abbey. I am so happy to finally meet you face to face." He, of course, says something similar: "It's so good to be here and to meet you, since I've heard so much about you."

If I had said, "Welcome to the abbey" but continued to talk, never giving him a chance to add a word one way or another, he would think, "Well, this monk is a very unusual person, a bit on the strange side." That would not be a good way to start building a friendship.

My friend and I can be present to one another in several ways. Obviously, we can be physically present, in the same place, the same room. We can also be intellectually present to one another, discussing politics or religion, or expressing other opinions and ideas. And we can be present to one another emotionally, laughing or crying together, experiencing joy or fear together. Real presence is active presence. It is not simply being with the other person. It is not a passive disposition, but an active, conscious response to the other person. It is a presence that requires us deliberately to direct ourselves toward the other person. When I am being present to someone, I physically face them, I look at them eye to eye, and I might lean slightly toward them with a look of anticipation. In real or active presence I am listening, anticipating, focusing on the other person's world. There is no pretending I care, faking my interest, or wishing they would hurry up so I can say what I want to say. Active presence is a deliberate movement toward the other person. I am seeking to focus myself on them, bringing what I have, finished or unfinished, into my response. I invite the other person to reveal themselves as they are, without masks or facades.

Real presence leads to the second element in a friendship: deep sharing. The exchange of thoughts, information, and life experiences build that relationship in such a way that the individuals come to know, respect, appreciate, and love each other in an ever deeper friendship. Friends must take turns being actively present with each other. When we become present to each other, we can share on a deeper level. Sure, we share all the time. We share materials; we share ideas and feelings. However, our lives need a deeper level of sharing at times. The question is whether we can accomplish that deeper kind of sharing that joins us spiritually. The sharing of more than the facts of our experiences, the sharing of our raw and honest experiences, is an essential part of our lives. It is the exchange of ideas, feelings, memories, and life experiences, with no cover-ups, no partial display, no falsities, and no repression or suppression.

None of us needs to be an open book all the time. I am not talking about sharing at this level continually. But deep sharing is essential in our lives. There are necessary moments when we need to share our experiences, without fear, with someone else. These moments of emotional nakedness build trust in others, in ourselves, and thus in the work that God is doing in our lives. Although this kind of growth may be painful at times, it is necessary. Deep sharing allows us to face our fears about others and about ourselves, and it allows us to confront shame and guilt, so that these crippling experiences can become less powerful in our daily lives.

The third important element of friendship, after presence and deep sharing, is self-sacrifice. Healthy friendship depends on each person's willingness to sacrifice for the good of the other person. To establish and carry out my presence with another, the kind we have been discussing, requires self-sacrifice. To build presence I must suspend my own needs at that moment, I must put aside what I want, what I crave, what I think I deserve, for the moment. My needs are as important as anyone else's, but getting them met does not require constant attention. By focusing on the needs of others I can create a space between my needs and myself. It is a space in which I am not in control. Letting go for a few moments or hours, tending to the needs of others, allows for God to work and always lets me know that I am not in charge. Self-sacrifice allows us to distance ourselves from our problems. Have you ever been working on something, trying to solve a problem, or studying for an exam and feeling like you are treading water, getting nowhere? What do you do? Sometimes we take a break; we let go for a little while. Often when we return to an activity or task we approach it with new vigor or new ideas. Progress often comes easier. Self-sacrifice is like this. When we practice self-sacrifice, we take the focus off our own problems for a while. During this time we may experience a rejuvenation, gain new ideas, or acquire a new perspective. Self-sacrifice serves both me and the other person. In temporarily giving up my needs and wants, I allow the other person that vital presence they need for sharing at a level that brings deeper understanding, deeper union, within themselves and with others. Self-sacrifice makes room for real, active presence and the possibility of deep meaningful sharing.

Presence, sharing, and self-sacrifice are the elements by which relationships are built. These are also the elements by which we build our prayer life. First, we need to be present to God. When people come for private retreats I ask them, "Why have you come to make this retreat? How may I help you?" Often their response is, "Father, you are a monk. Teach me to pray." Prayer, as I have said, is presence, so I invite them to go to our Blessed Sacrament Chapel and to be before the Lord for forty-five minutes. They say, "Well, that's fine. What do you want me to do there?" I say to them, "Just be." They say, "Yes, I heard you, but isn't there a Scripture text that I might use, a Psalm, or maybe a spiritual book with a chapter—a page or two that you might want me to read and ponder?" I answer, "No. Just be. Be there before God." I'm talking about the whole person being there, their thoughts, their feelings, their instincts, everything—right there, before the Lord.

So the retreatant goes to the chapel, and during the first twenty minutes wonders, "What's going on here? I'm not comfortable with this." They are distracted by all the noises of activities going on outside. The person shifts from one side to another and wonders, "What am I doing here? This is the most foolish thing I have ever done." It's pretty much the rule; twenty minutes into that forty-five–minute experience, the person is overwhelmingly frustrated and is ready to leave the chapel. They wonder once more, "Why am I here?" And all of a sudden they begin to hear the answer: "I'm here to be in God's presence." Then they settle down, becoming inwardly quiet, and the world around them disappears. For the next twenty minutes, or so, they are ecstatic. Maybe for the first time in their life, they have experienced what it means to be with God.

At this point the retreatant is ready for that sharing with God, because God has spoken already. The prayer book of the Church is the Holy Scripture, the Bible. It is the story of God's love for us and our response to that Love— God's love and forgiveness, our faithfulness, unfaithfulness, repentance, rededication—the whole cycle that runs throughout the Scriptures, all of which reflects our own spiritual journey. In this sharing, it is important that we learn to search the Scriptures to understand God, understand ourselves, and understand our relationship with God, with the self, and with others in our lives.

One way of letting God speak to us through the Scriptures is through *lectio divina*, a method from my own Benedictine tradition that has become popular today. Benedict would have us, as monks, begin from the Word of God and return to the Word of God every day as the basis of our day and as the basis of every step in our journey. *Lectio divina* is a means of reading the Word of God, meditating on that Word, praying that Word, and letting that word affect us.

In the Benedictine tradition of *lectio divina,* we start by doing four readings of the same text. First, we simply read the words of the text, slowly and carefully. The second time, we read to find the emphasis in the text. The third time, we read to find out what the author is trying to convey to us. And in the fourth reading, we ask ourselves, What does this mean to me? That is real reading of the Scripture.

In the second part of *lectio divina*, following the four readings of the text, we meditate on what we have read— that is, turning it over again and again in our minds. For example, Jesus says, "A new commandment I give you, that you love one another as I have loved you." We can ponder that endlessly.

We then move to the third part of *lectio*, which is to pray about the Word, that it might be a reality in our lives, so that we learn to love one another as he has loved us, until we are filled with grace from this Word of God, the gift of the Spirit.

Finally, we contemplate and rest in that Scripture, completely immersed in the Word letting that Word form and transform our lives. This is the Benedictine way of prayer. This is our way of dialoguing with God.

When I look to the Scripture as a way of God speaking to me in my personal, private prayer, how do I respond? I respond from where I am at a given moment. I might respond by words or by feelings. I might respond in many different ways. My heart tells me how to respond.

If your best friend comes to meet you, would you want that friend to say to you, "Now, here is a text, and here is the way we are going to visit?" You would say, "That's foolish," and you would be right. Just as we would speak to our friend, we speak to God simply from the fullness of our heart, where we are, which has been touched deeply by God's Word. "If today you hear the voice of the Lord, harden not your hearts…"

Many times, at night after a hard full day, I stop by the chapel to spend a few minutes in prayer. If I picked up a book, I would probably drop it. To be with the Lord and thank him for the day by just being there is the perfect prayer because that is where I am at that point in the day.

The third element of relationship, self-sacrifice, is also essential in our relationship with God. As we become present to God, listening for the Word of God and then allowing that Word to transform us, we grow in our desire to lay down our life and follow him, as Jesus calls us to do. This means taking up our cross daily and denying the self so that we might go through that conversion that is the ultimate meaning of our life on this earth. This is a lifelong process, one conversion after another, after another, as the Word of God becomes part of us and calls us to lay down our self-centeredness, to die to the self, and to rise to new life in Christ Jesus.

Each of us develops our own unique prayer style, because each person is a unique gift of God and has a unique relationship with God. An excellent way to discern our own pattern of prayer is by keeping a journal. It also helps build some accountability into our spiritual life. I feel that journal keeping is absolutely necessary for calling ourselves to account for this most important relationship in our life each day. We can use a journal to record each day whether we spent time in prayer and perhaps the Scripture that we used for prayer. We can also record one thought that describes our experience in prayer that day, a thought that becomes our spiritual food for that day. Doing this consistently, every day for a month or two months, six months, or a year, helps us grow in our prayer life.

Sometimes the written word helps me to organize my thoughts. I mentioned in an earlier chapter that I sometimes suggest to directees that they write a letter to God, but I also find it helpful at times to do this myself. I write a friendly letter to God about my relationship to him, and I allow myself to say whatever I want to say to God as my best friend. I share the positives as well as the negatives in my life, even though he knows them already. I tell him my concerns and what I am looking for in my relationship with him, what I expect from him. I also let him know how I have been satisfied or disappointed in our relationship. Then I leave it up to him in prayer to respond. If you choose to do this exercise, I also suggest sharing your letter with your spiritual director as a way to get in closer touch with your spiritual journey, especially with your prayer life.

The letter to God is a form of journaling, and any form of journaling can be an excellent tool to help us reflect on the love of God as it is forming and transforming our lives day after day. From that we will know our giftedness, our call in life. In bringing these things to spiritual direction and sharing them with our director, we can determine the answers to the ultimate questions in our journey: Who are we, what are we, and where are we in our relationship with God? With faithfulness and consistency in our prayer life, these questions are answered in wonderful ways.

Prayer is the way to discipleship, to a deeper relationship with Jesus. As in Mark's Gospel, we are called to be his companions and then to preach or to carry on his ministry. So it is most important, then, that we look at our prayer life as the absolutely necessary foundation of our life—our spiritual lives, our growth in God's love, our growth in our relationship with Jesus, with the Father and the Spirit, and then in our relationships with each other

Key Ideas: Prayer is not something we do, but is a relationship. Our relationship/friendship with God is no different than any other relationship. There are some essential elements in any "friendship." It too requires our effort to be present, to share of our self, and yes, on occasion, to sacrifice our wishes and needs. This type of deep-sharing allows us to face our own fears, our weaknesses, and our shame. In sharing these facets of our spiritual journey with God and others, we build relationship. Through our relationships we come to conversion..."the ultimate meaning of our life on earth." What are the elements that make your most significant relationship (i.e. wife, best friend, father, etc.) meaningful and fulfilling for you? Compare this relationship to your relationship with God. How might you integrate the qualities of your significant relationship and your meaningful and fulfilling for you? Compare this relationship to your relationship with God. How might you integrate the qualities of your significant relationship and your relationship with God? In what ways do you make yourself present? How often do you share the personal things in your life with God? What are you being called to sacrifice so as to deepen your relationship with God?

1. Edward J. Farrell *Prayer Is a Hunger*
(Dimension Books, 1972).

Friendship

As the old adage goes, "Tell me who your friends are, and I'll tell you who you are." How very true it is that our friendships form us in the journey of life at any given time or place. We cannot walk our journey without significant friendships. To the degree that we have true friends, we grow in our relationship with God, with ourselves, and with those who travel the journey with us.

I have a stack of photo albums that I always enjoy looking at. As I turn page after page and spend some precious moments with the pictures in the albums, I recognize a deep conviction about the friendships that have changed me and formed me. It all started in the family—those relationships that form us from day one. I was the third of four sons born to Irish and German parents during the hard times of the Great Depression and Prohibition. My parents taught my brothers and me to be hardworking, industrious, and fiercely competitive individuals. In our home, faith was taught by example rather than by words.

My uncle was a priest. Possibly he had an early influence on my dream of someday becoming a priest. One photo shows me at about age seven standing by an altar made by my uncle, who was a contractor. I was dressed in priestly vestments made for me by a Benedictine brother at St. Meinrad. I was encouraged in my dream of becoming a priest, and I sometimes wondered later if my vocation was not more the dream of my mother rather than my own call from God. But as my life progressed, I became aware of what God was calling me uniquely to do.

I entered seminary in 1943. I have before me a picture of my class—sixty young high school freshmen. What a happy bunch we were! The first obstacle to the priesthood was Latin because it was the most difficult course. And I will never forget one of the teachers who formed me, saying to our Latin class, "If ten of you become ordained priests, you will be above average." Of course, we thanked him for such positive affirmation because in those days there were so many candidates that there had to be a process of weeding us out. The seminary was an obstacle course and if you survived, you were ordained. By the way, of the sixty freshmen, exactly ten of us were ordained twelve years later throughout the world and in various dioceses and religious orders.

Those years in the seminary were filled with many friendships, much fun, and some pain, such as when a good friend left the seminary to go his own way. But all through that time each friend had a definite impact. Even to this day, those of us who are still left—the number is becoming fewer—can sit down and recall the many stories and happy times we had together. More than we realized, God worked in us and through us as he prepared us to do his work, so that we would reach the full potential he had given each of us in his time and his way.

Early in my career I met one of the persons who was to influence, and continues to influence, my life today. That was my spiritual director, a man of many gifts. He had the ability to draw the best out of a person. So for the next eleven years until I was ordained a priest, and ever since then, he has been an inspiration, a man of vision, a true friend.

What often draws two people into friendship is an attraction to a common interest. It is helpful to look at our values, what we hold to be important. When we find someone who has the same values, the same interests, we have a good basis for beginning a friendship in which we draw closer and share more deeply.

One of my close friends is a person who, like me, loves books. Not surprisingly, we met in a bookstore looking at books about, of all things, friendship. From that chance meeting we began to talk about friendship. We went on meeting and talking and growing in our friendship because there were many areas of life we could share and enjoy. In many ways we were the same, but there were definite ways in which we were, and are, and always will be, different. That is what contributed to the richness of our friendship over the years.

Both in our friendship with God and our friendships with each other, we grow in presence—being present to our friends physically, emotionally, and spiritually. This is the deepest foundation for any genuine friendship. The ability to be present to each other develops slowly, just as the ability to trust each other develops throughout the friendship. After presence comes the sharing. Here again, this is very gradual. It doesn't happen the first time we meet a person How many times people can know each other for years and not touch certain parts of each other's life until they have the opportunity to share. Through presence and through this sharing, a bond of love and friendship develops that leads a person to the sacrifice of self for the good of the other. This is what true love is about.

If you asked me today, "How important is friendship?" I would tell you that next to God friendship is the most important thing, because as I mentioned in an earlier chapter, Jesus said, "This is my commandment: love one another, as I have loved you" (John 15:12). And at another time he said to his followers, "You are my friends, if you do what I command you... I call you friends, because I have made known to you everything I have learned from my Father" (John 15:15). Jesus called us into this very special relationship with him, with the Father, and with the Spirit to show us the way we are to relate to each other on a deeper level.

I learned the meaning of friendships after my move to California. In our new community, when I reached out for the supports that I had known before, they were not there. For the first time I felt the pain of having no close friends nearby. My own needs for intimacy were not being met in my new situation, and I began to understand the power and the necessity of close friendships.

In our community we had many good times, but we also had to struggle in the work of founding a new community. Although it was going well enough, there was something missing. I had to ask myself, What is really important to me? What are the values that make me, me? What would I enjoy sharing with others? And, How can I find friends—people who would understand me as I understand them?

Early in my ministry in California, I got into youth leadership work because that is where I felt challenged and energized. Spiritual direction and leadership are two values that are deeply imbedded in my personality, and I always look forward to finding others who can understand my deep love for these gifts. But for the first time in my life I was alone and I felt alone. I had to stand on my own two feet, think for myself, decide for myself, and walk in the conviction that comes from a sense of knowing who I really am. At the time, the other confrere was certainly a help because he always went one way if I went the other, which forced me to stand alone. This freed me up and freed him up. However, it was a process, because feeling all right with being alone and independent was critical to realizing my deeper identity and the intimacy to which God was calling me.

With that aloneness came a loneliness. Often we hear of people who are desperately afraid of being lonely. Well, everyone is lonely; it is a part of the human condition. For me, it was an invitation to pray. I am only as alone as I want to be. God is always there. God does not go away. We might go away from God, but he is always there. Therefore, the loneliness, this passage that I was in, was important for me to come to know who I was and who I am.

The only thing I knew that I had to avoid, because it is not in me, was isolation. God had put many people around me, fine people, who were potentially good friends. One or two eventually became deeply spiritual friends. It is through that kind of friendship that I came to know who I was. I was then able to enter into that close relationship that is so rewarding spiritually and emotionally.

Often it is through a mutual acquaintance that we begin a friendship. Robert J. Wicks, in his book *Seeds of Sensitivity*[1], says that the qualities in which true friendship begins and grows are those that allow us to learn as well as to give, to share as well as to guide, to be unique as well as to have things in common, and to seek all that can be sought rather than to hold each other back in fear.

When we realize that the best way to define prayer is as a relationship, and that the best of relationships is found in friendship, so the qualities of a life-giving friendship, one that changes the lives of those who are involved in such a relationship, are qualities that flow from one's relationship to God—one's prayer. These same qualities flow into one's relationship with our significant others.

Years ago we put together a retreat program called The Search for Christian Maturity, for the purpose of supporting young people's need for acceptance and affirmation during the difficult years of growing up, as they searched for who they were and what they wanted. That retreat program was one of the first-ever youth-to-youth apostolates developed in recent years. The young people who participated became alive with excitement. Their energy seemed boundless in response to having some of their deepest needs touched—needs that never had been addressed, particularly about growth and faith. We put the program together based on the real questions that everyone asks as they walk their journey. Until those questions are satisfied, the search continues for an answer, for a meaning to life, because in this meaning is found a vocation, whether it means walking the journey with a significant other in one's life, or going alone and giving one's self completely to God's work with the help of the gift of celibacy. It was a wonderful experience to work with these young people, who were obviously very gifted. Today, some thirty years later, they are doing extremely well, for the most part, in living up to the expectations that were placed on them.

The powerful part of that experience was that it was a program of spiritual direction, in which we walked with those young people, respecting them as gifted individuals who were anxious to change the world but who realized they must first come to know themselves. In that program, relationships developed. Those of us who served as spiritual directors were encouraged as we learned to listen, to affirm the young participants, and to support them in living the Gospel, so that they would break out of the self-centeredness of their childhood to go through the confusion of adolescence and into young adulthood, and then into whatever vocation they felt was God's call. The young people, in turn, were then able to go out and do the same for others. To this day, those young people still come back and love to call to mind the memories of the challenges—the weekends, the moments—in their journey that changed their lives, because they were experiencing good direction and good companionship. This is a vital step in the spiritual journey and in spiritual maturity.

Each time we had a Search weekend the pattern was the same. Young people were forced by their parents or a parish priest to go on the Search weekend. They came in protest, looking for nothing except a way to leave. What they expected was a completely negative experience in which they would be lectured and told what to do, one more exercise much like school, which they often resented.

Much to their surprise, they were made to feel important, unique, and worth listening to. We let them know that they are important and that they could express themselves. We even gave them permission not to be perfect. They became themselves and began to discover what a real relationship to God and each other was, and what real friendship was. They began to forget their prejudices; they entered into, and took up, the leadership. Rather than fighting not to come, they began fighting to be a part of that program. The result was that they became the leaders among their own peers, willing to speak for what they believed, willing to stand for something. Many of them developed friendships that took them through that difficult time in their life.

On the Search weekend, the young people faced several basic questions: Who am I? What do we mean by "community?" Why do we need one another? What is the challenge in today's world to live worthwhile lives? When the young people went home, they felt ready to go out and change the world. Most important, they got a first glimpse of what life is really about: the inner journey. It is not about being egocentric, about being number one. It is instead about laying down our lives so that others might live, and so that the world becomes a better place.

A real friend supports us and draws out the best in us. It is through friendships that we come to know ourselves—who we are, what we are, and where we are. The older we get, the more acquaintances and fewer friends we might accumulate. However, the quality of the friendships deepens.

Three common issues that friends address and work through together, usually in adolescence or young adulthood are: sexuality, career, and relationship with God. The young adult may come to realize that their sexuality is a gift from God given to fulfill the very purpose for which God created him or her—to love and to love deeply and, if God so wills, to have a family and enter into that work of art of raising children according to God's designs. Or they might take this gift of love and forego the support of marriage and, with the gift of celibacy, give their whole life to God's people. To love, and love deeply, in both cases, taking the same gift of God and using it for God's glory by helping others, is how we fulfill God's purpose for us.

As the spiritual director, the companion on the journey, listens to each person describe the significant others in their lives, their friendships, including their spiritual friendships, the person comes to know God's will, because God's will is written in the people in our lives, as well as in the events and in our personalities. Jesus said, "Where two or more are gathered in my name, there I am in their midst" (Matthew 18:20). Over a lifetime, as we pray and reflect about our friendships with the help of a companion on the journey, we find the power of spiritual companionship, which we also call spiritual direction.

In the relationship of spiritual direction, the Holy Spirit works not only through the director to the person seeking direction, but from that person back to the director. It is as important to receive as it is to give, even if we are ministering to others. We must not only give charitably, but we must receive gracefully. By receiving gracefully we are actually giving; we are giving the other person a moment to give the gift of giving. Friendship must be mutual and equal in the give-and-take process, because mutuality leads to interpersonal and intrapersonal development and spiritual growth. Deep friendship, built on trust, respect, personal space, and boundaries, are opportunities for growing personally and for discovering God's great love for us.

If you've written your own story, as I suggested in an earlier chapter, I invite you now to go back to your story. Consider the significant people in your life, both positive and negative, and ask yourself, "What are the most important characteristics of a healthy friendship—a friendship that gives life to both individuals?"

Then reflect on the significant people who have walked with you in your journey. Some of those people may have become significant because they changed your life just as you changed theirs as the two of you shared your deeper self. Friendship, the type that forms our journey, does not develop through a one-time meeting. It grows through ups and downs and becomes progressively stronger. As it grows, it meets our basic need for someone to listen to us, accept us, affirm us, and support us throughout our journey of life. We cannot walk the journey alone.

Key Ideas: "Where two or more are gathered in my name, there I am in their midst {Matt.18:20}." God's words tell us that friendship is essential in our spiritual journey. In our friendships (two or more), Our Father declares His presence to us. This is a specific promise of Himself when we gather with the significant others in our lives. "Next to God, friendship is the most important thing." Jesus surrounded himself with friends (Disciples) as he journeyed to reveal His Father's calling in his life. God speaks to us in silence, however, He also utilizes others to mirror, affirm, and support our calling. God's will for us is written in the events and relationships in our lives. Take the time to reflect on your most significant friendships. Identify the values you seek in others and examine these "companionships" for the evidence of God's will for you. Your Spiritual Director can be most helpful in this process.

1. Robert J. Wicks, *Seeds of Sensitivity: Deepening Your Spiritual Life* (Notre Dame, Indiana: Ave Maria Press, 1995).

Family

Ｗe often see and hear today that the family is in crisis. We are challenged in every way to rediscover what a real family and real community are.

The family is the foundation, the starting point of our personal journey. For that reason in spiritual direction it is important and often revealing for a person to describe their family—the love and friendship they experienced in their family and the relationships among the various members of the family.

We do well each Advent season to reflect on the foundation, the family, in which Jesus began his earthly journey. Like many families in the world today, the Holy Family—Jesus, Mary, and Joseph—as we find them in the Gospel story, were refugees. Family life depends, as we know, not only on houses and possessions, but more important, on the mutual love and friendship that binds the members together and keeps them together.

Some years ago when I spent a three-month sabbatical in contemplative prayer, I discovered that another participant in the program was from my home town; in fact, his family had lived next door to mine. Whenever we had the opportunity to chat, he told me stories about my family members that I knew nothing about because I was away at the monastery or the seminary when those events took place. Hearing those stories helped me to reflect further on how my family was the foundation of my spiritual journey.

Many people today are looking at the foundation of their journey—their families. More and more, they are asking: "What is a family? What is a real community?" The description I have found to be most helpful is that the family is a community of individuals who are bound together by common values and yet who are all different from each other. It is a unity from diversity. Both unity and diversity must be respected and affirmed at all times. Herein lies the secret of a strong family life that gives a firm stable foundation for the journey of life.

Today, one of the truly hope-filled signs related to family is the existence, and the number, of support groups. Support group is the modern manifestation of community and the modern need for community if we are to grow and to change our lives. In support groups, people from diverse backgrounds and with diverse personalities come together, usually with a common goal, and learn to build trust by respecting and affirming each other.

Respect and affirmation become possible when there is communication. What creates and sustains the bond, the love, that keeps the family, or the community, together is the art of communication. In the context of the Church, we often hear the term excommunication, meaning the act of cutting someone off, or cutting oneself off, from this energy and affirmation. Communication is based on some important virtues that help to develop family relationships. The first virtue is the total acceptance of each individual, wherever that individual is at any given moment in their personal unique journey. This acceptance calls for tolerance. It is easy for us to tell everyone else who they should be, and in so doing, without realizing it, reject who they really are. When that happens they do the very same thing to us. They tell us who we are supposed to be and that they will not accept us unless we are what we are called to be.

From tolerance comes the second virtue that keeps communication alive: patience. A family is patient enough to provide the time and space for a person to grow and change. Patience also makes it possible for the family to affirm the person's process of growth and change. Without patience, this isn't possible. We can all think back to times in our lives when we were going to change. Life is not about simply being. Life is not static; it is dynamic. It is always changing. What is good in us is, hopefully, becoming better, and what is better is getting close to the best we can do. We then recognize, once again, that what is in us is good and that we want to patiently become better. As with prayer, we need a sacred time and a sacred space for this process, because that is where we can grow and change. That is also where we receive the affirmation to grow and change.

The family is where we can call out the best in each other, not the worst. It is true that "I'll be as good or as bad as you call me to be." It is a matter of compliment versus criticism. It is so easy to criticize each other, and that negativity stops communication and growth, breaking down the bond of friendship that is the basis of family life.

The final virtue that communication is based on is forgiveness. In the family there has to be forgiveness and acceptance again and again. We all need forgiveness many times each day. The degree to which we are able to forgive others determines the level of our communication. The less we forgive and the less tolerant we are, the more difficult it becomes for any real bonding to occur in the family.

It is the Father's will that we grow in Christian holiness through the friction and tension that are a part of every family life. Even the Holy Family experienced it. In his Gospel St. Luke speaks of the tension, patience, and forgiveness that occurred after Mary and Joseph lost Jesus in Jerusalem and spent three days searching for him. When we all practice patience, tolerance, and merciful forgiveness in loving, giving, and selfless ways, our family life becomes a place where we can grow in our love for God and for others.

God's presence is at the heart of the family. The love of Jesus keeps us together because we pray together. We often pray together the Lord's Prayer, the prayer in which Jesus taught us how we are to relate to his Father, to ourselves, and to each other. We can also pray together before meals. For example: "God indeed is with us. Lord, give us the light through the example of your family, and guide our feet to the way of peace. Amen." Earlier in this book I spoke of being present to God by having a sacred time and a sacred space for prayer. I spoke also of the sharing of *lectio divina*, or the reading of the Scriptures, and of sacrificing our own wants for the good of someone else. As in family life, so in community life, whether in the Church or in a religious community, a commitment to community, like a commitment to prayer, grows through presence, sharing, and self-sacrifice.

First and most important, in the foundation of community life is presence—physical, emotional, and spiritual presence to each other. Some years ago, it was my turn to preach a homily at the monastery. The text for that day was Matthew 19:1-6, where Jesus is speaking about marriage: "What God has united, man must not divide." So here I was, about to speak to a group of celibates on a text that seemed at first sight not to apply. But once I started thinking about community, I realized that just as it certainly applies to the relationship of husband and wife—the friendship that draws them together and is the foundation of the family—so it is the very same relationship that draws us together and makes the foundation of community. When God draws us together into community, be it family, religious community, working community, ministry, or whatever other grouping in which we are pursuing a common endeavor with each other's help, God is the one who forms community. We may be asking ourselves, "Why did God call me into a relationship with this community?" But God knows what he is doing, and he makes no mistakes, even though it may take us a lifetime to find the answer to our question. "What God has joined together..."—God calls a community together, he knows each one of us, and he put us together for our sanctification. When we come, someday, to the end of our journey we will understand the mystery of our calling to a deep relationship with God. We will also understand our calling to walk our journey in community and to find our support, our challenge to grow, as we try day by day to live community life, especially to be present.

There are many situations in which we can find a reason to excuse ourselves. Our belonging to a community then becomes simply a matter of words, far from the reality that comes only with the day-by-day, 24-hours-a-day, seven days a week experience. So, presence, as painful as it can be at times, or as joyful and supportive as it can be at other times, is the all-important foundation of a community, where we can find the kind of support we are meant to receive from living in community.

Years ago at Prince of Peace Abbey we had an experience of community that we all will remember for a long time. The abbey is situated on Benet Hill, overlooking the San Luis Rey Valley, with the San Luis Rey River running through it. At that time we had three wet winters, which were unusual for dry Southern California. As a result, the San Luis Rey River at the foot of our hill, which is normally a dry bed and provides an Arizona crossing to the local town, became a raging river. Our community, including those who must access the local area to do the shopping, was marooned. Our whole community had to stay home for nearly two weeks. The only way out was by foot or by helicopter. During that time, everyone relaxed in the fact that there was no place else to go. Throughout those two weeks, we came to know the concept of community, the silence, the quiet, and the power of presence as we had never sensed before in our abbey. We look back to that experience as a fond memory and a time of spiritual growth.

The second way that a commitment to community grows is through sharing. This sharing must take place in many different areas. One area is in community prayer with those whom we have been called to share and to walk the journey. We need to celebrate our togetherness by prayer. It is by prayer that we are able to realize God's presence and power, which is especially manifested in our oneness and togetherness as community.

Another area where sharing must take place is in work. When we work for others, when we dedicate our efforts on behalf of others, we develop spiritual discipline. We develop maturity and commitment in our actions. We learn to sacrifice some of who we are (or think we are), in order to discover more of who we are meant to be in the eyes of God. Work can discipline us mentally, physically, and spiritually. Work gives us structure, focus for our behaviors, and meaning for our actions. Our work, whatever it may be, can symbolize our commitment to others. Work can help us to get outside ourselves and live more objectively in relation to others. Our commitment to our work, and especially the sharing that we do in our work, can develop in us in a larger commitment to our community and to God. Work is one aspect of our reality that grounds us in this way of truth.

It is important not only that we pray and work together as a means of sharing, but also that we play together. If all we ever do in our community is work, we have only part of a full life, not the whole, because all work and no play makes for a dull community life. Our culture is given to workaholism. We are taught that the more we do, the better we are. Yet, if we pray together, work together, and play together, we can keep a sense of our community, our bondedness, our care for each other, very much alive. We get to see parts of each other's personality that we might not see in a day-by-day work environment.

This sharing must happen in community, or meetings,

where we sit down and really talk through issues. There is no family or group that does not have times of challenges because of differences, since we all have different personalities. The only way these differences can be turned into channels of grace is by our willingness, with God's help, to confront issues, as difficult as they might be. To fear confrontation is to go into deeper levels of denial. If there is a strong identity and a loving acceptance of each member in the community as well as of the community as a whole, it is because its members see confrontation as good and necessary at times. It is an art to be learned by patient practice. Feelings are much healthier when they are shared at the table than when they are bottled up inside us, waiting to explode. Repressed feelings are not good for us or for others and can lead to bitterness and complaining—things that tear at the fiber of good communication and good healthy community life. And in healthy confrontation, we learn how to listen to each other. The more we listen, the more we come to appreciate others, and the more they become open to the idea of listening to us.

At the heart of our journey lies self-sacrifice, the third and final way that a commitment to community, or family, grows. As we commit ourselves to self-sacrifice for the greater good of others, we learn the way of the cross. Christ says when we die to our self, when we lose our self, we will find it. Those who die shall live, and those who are first shall be last. When we limit our wants, our desires, our way, we free ourselves to discover the deeper meaning of who we are. As we struggle to give of ourselves to something larger than ourselves (others, family, community), in other words die to our self, we learn to see our self with greater clarity. Self-indulgence narrows our view in life and restricts our access to others. It is through others that we come to know our self, adjust our self, change our self. The mirroring that others provide us is an opportunity for growth and healing. This dimension of human life is critical to healthy and true living.

Presence, sharing, and self-sacrifice are the foundation stones that help us discern what is good for the community. These attributes remind us that there are times in the community when we must learn what it means to be selfless. There is always a give and a take in community life. Tensions are a reality, and they are good when they are kept manageable through communication and sharing. As we become more aware of these foundation stones for true community life, and quietly practice them day by day, we help build a community life that is a strong and life-giving support in our life's journey.

Here are the constants in genuine community life:
- We must each learn who we are and from where we are coming.
- We must invest time and energy in building trust and honesty. This includes a willingness to share, and to share more deeply, as appropriate.
- We must grow in our awareness of what we bring to our community, not just what we are looking for from the community.
- We must grow in our awareness of God's power and presence in our community, as wonderful or as painful as it can be at any given time.

In community life, as in marriage and family life, we are called to change and change again, in an ongoing conversion. We do that with God's help, with our own gifts and talents, and with the support of others.

Key Ideas: The family is our first experience of community. All community comes from God, and it is here that God teaches us to love in and through mutuality in friendship, and in self-sacrifice. Through community we discover our values and are provided the arena in which to exercise and hone them. Our community life, whether in a family or religious community, develops our acceptance, tolerance, patience, and forgiveness with others and our self. Through the tension, friction, and pain of our communal relationships, God forms us according to His will. What are the most significant "communities" that you share in? What do you bring to these communities? What do you expect to receive? Are you meeting others needs and getting your needs met as God intends you to? Where are you being called to grow, or to sacrifice of yourself? The answers to these questions can deepen our understanding of who we are, and what God's purpose is for us.

Chapter 9

Surrender

From my youth I was taught that to surrender is to be defeated. It was drilled into me that where there is a will, there is a way, and it is better to die trying to get your own way than to surrender.

The suffering and death of Jesus on the cross was thought to be his total failure. His enemies, those who had persecuted him, had apparently won. We have come to realize, however, that the opposite is true. Here is the victory of Christ. His victory is in the surrender of his will to the will of his heavenly Father. It is this surrender that can change and transform our life's journey.

The truly great people are those who are very gifted but who surrender their own will to the will of the God. We can look among our closest friends and acquaintances, even at the outstanding people in the world today, those recognized universally as being great, and see that their greatness stems from their willingness to surrender to the love of God who calls them to follow his example—that is, to lay down their life for others.

In front of the seminary where I was a student in the 1940s is a Celtic cross made of sandstone. On the base of that cross is a Latin word that sums up the whole meaning of our lives: *Sacrificabo* ("I will sacrifice"). Our journey to the Father is always in Jesus and in the power of the Holy Spirit. We are to be one with Jesus. As the Apostle Paul says,

"I live now not with my own life but with the life of Christ who lives in me" (Galatians 2:20).

Quite by accident, it was my good fortune some years ago to spend time with Mother Theresa of Calcutta in Tijuana at the Missionaries of Charity Seminary. Here I was, in a very plain room with a person who was world renowned and who had an impressive presence and much power. We stood face to face and prayed. She stood there, obviously in total surrender to God's will in her life. She had but one ambition: to have Christ in her, and through her to reach out to the poorest of the poor of her brothers and sisters.

As we prayed, I thought of the story of the sons of Zebedee and their ambitious mother, who approaches Jesus, asking that her sons be placed next to Jesus, one on his right and the other on his left, when he comes into his kingdom. Jesus answers the request with two other questions, which touch the heart of our lives. He asks each of us, whatever our state in life, the same questions: "Do you know what you are asking? Can you drink the cup that I am going to drink?" (Matthew 20:22).

The fullness of discipleship means that each day we must surrender to the Father's will as it unfolds in our lives. The cross and the suffering are at the very core of the journey. Just as Jesus made his way to Jerusalem to carry out his Father's will to the last drop of his precious blood on the cross, we too are to journey in surrender to the Father's will. Surrender was central to the journey of Jesus on this earth, and so it is for all of us.

The family or the community with whom we walk the journey—be they special friends, significant others, or relatives—is where this surrender is to shine forth. This is because we have come to do nothing but to love Christ and to imitate him and his surrender to the Father's will.

We live in an age when people profess, "I'm here to do what I want!" What it comes down to is, "I'm here to do what I want" versus "Christ living in me and through me." The latter approach is the healthy way of being one's self, laying down one's life and taking up the cross. Jesus said that unless we deny ourselves daily, take up our cross, and follow him, we cannot be his disciples (Luke 14:26). We are called to be ourselves and then to die and rise in the closest union with Christ. One follows the other.

During my vacation, I always look forward to spending time with my brothers and their children. One time I was asked to watch the children while my brother and sister-in-law went out for an hour or so. I thought this would be a wonderful experience. The minute the parents walked out the door, all six children scattered in different directions and pandemonium set in. By the time their parents returned, I began to realize what real surrender is all about. I came to appreciate their vocation and how beautifully they live it. This became a renewed inspiration for me to be faithful to my own vocation.

As we look upon the crucified Master, the Lord we have come to follow, we begin to see true surrender at its deepest level: the denial of one's self. At times in our lives there is an unconscious opposition, a struggle going on between God's way and our way. We may feel that because we have studied theology or read extensively we have a good grasp of God's will as it is expressed in the day-to-day activities of our lives. Yet, God has a particular plan for us: to be like Jesus. As Jesus died and rose again, we also die and rise again. We are called to walk with Christ in his footsteps. We are called to be like him, to act like him, to love like him, and ultimately to die to ourselves like him, so that we can rise like him. Our dying and rising occurs every time we choose to sacrifice ourselves, to give to another, to allow someone else to be first. In each moment of sacrifice, in dying to the self, we allow God to re-create in us the death-resurrection process. We may die to something we want to do, something we envy, something we want to possess.

In rejecting our self-indulgence we die to the self, surrendering the self to God and freeing the self from the worldly elements that surround us.

To discern this truth, we must learn to listen in prayer, listen to what is going on in our lives, and listen to the significant people in our lives. It is important to have someone help us hear the things we need to hear, and face the things we don't want to face. The spiritual direction experience is one in which the director mirrors the life story of the person he directs, back to the him. This process enables the individual to see more clearly their life's journey and to understand further the will of God in their life. As I mentioned earlier, we need relationships and communion with others in order to know ourselves and to know God. The spiritual direction experience is an intense one-to-one relationship that helps the individual to see their story more clearly and honestly, and thus embrace it more completely, leading to greater oneness with the self and greater oneness with the Father. Throughout our life's journey God reveals to us our personal and unique story through our daily activities, relationships, and experiences. God is the author of our life, the editor of our story. The spiritual direction experience reflects the Father-son or Father-daughter relationship we have with God. Spiritual direction is an active process, a deliberate search for the truth in one's life. We must know our story, embrace it, and surrender it to God. Outside this process, in our daily lives, we must also seek and come to know this story. The significant others who pass through our life are critical to our understanding of this story. They are mirrors, often revealing God's authorship in our journey.

Surrender is a process, and an important part of that process is the sharing that brings about the surrender. It is much simpler to do what we are told unquestioningly, but that is not virtue. Sharing means to give and to take—vulnerability, surrender—the way to the "little" death and resurrection. Often, we may state our opinion on an issue we feel deeply about, and then when those in authority disagree or decide otherwise, we get upset and are quick to say that they don't really listen. But we need to look at authority from the other side. Power is meant to meet the needs of those whom we are serving. Power is given for service. Those who have power and who exercise authority have the obligation to use that authority to meet the needs of others. Authority is not given for the personal aggrandizement of the one in authority.

It is consoling to know that Christ himself struggled with authority in his agony in the Garden of Gethsemane—"Father, if it be possible, let this chalice," or this surrender, "pass from me, but not my will, Your will be done." And we know what happened. Did the Father's will change? No. Jesus accepted his suffering and his death because it was the will of his Father. The surrendering Jesus, then, is before us as a suffering servant, there to meet our every need and to lay down his life that we might live.

Authority is given for service, and like Christ we also are called to be servants. But at all human levels, authority is weak. God intended that relationship be founded on unconditional love, but human nature does not always comply. Others have been placed in authority over us— government, law enforcement, the judicial system, our bosses, and so on—and like Christ we must surrender to that authority. Christ ultimately surrendered his life under the authority of the Jews and Romans. However, the ultimate authority in our lives is God, and through faith we must discern the authorities over us. Just as Jesus challenged the authorities of his time, we too may be called to confront the powers over us, and we must actively discern when God is calling us to challenge authority. When injustice is evident we must discern our place and action. While God calls us to show tolerance and forgiveness in our relationships, and while surrender of our self is an essential element of our journey, the cross of earthly reality is that people in authority sometimes misuse their power over others. Consequently, there may be times when we are called to stand against the abuse of power and authority, just as Jesus did in the temple with the money-changers. While we are on earth, the finality of our journey may be in the hands of others or in something else, but our surrender to God ultimately brings us under his authority, to the Cross, and to our own death and resurrection. That surrender is what makes us one with the surrendering Christ.

In the Gospel of John, Jesus says to Peter, "When you were young you put on your own belt and walked where you liked; but when you grow old you will stretch out your hands, and somebody else will put a belt around you and take you where you would rather not go" (John 21:18). This is the true pattern of our lives. Surrender in the beginning may be easy, but eventually we come to that time in our lives when there is a death, a resurrection, and a total conversion. We break into a whole new and deeper relationship with Jesus. And not only with him, but also with those we are called to travel alongside on this journey. That death is something we should keep before us, realizing it will come. Each time we celebrate the Eucharist we commemorate the death and resurrection of the Lord, our Salvation. We sacrifice—*sacrificabo*—our own will, our own desires, for the sake of doing God's will. This sacrifice transforms us and brings about an ever closer union with Jesus in the Father's will and the great grace of the Holy Spirit. The sacrifice is renewed and a deeper communion comes from partaking of the body and blood of Christ.

The Lord is present in a special way in our moments of self-sacrifice. We minister in the way we give. We make God's love and God's care present in the lives of others by our self-sacrifice. In this sacrifice is the power of the great virtue of surrender. Christ lives in each one of us as we serve him by giving to the sick, the poor, the visitor, all who come to us in need. We make Christ present. In this presence of Christ is our unity, the ultimate reconciliation through the daily celebration and living of the Eucharist. The daily Eucharist is the gift of ourselves, that Jesus may transform us into himself.

Key Ideas: Surrender can transform our life, and is the essence of our spiritual journey. Our surrendering must manifest itself in our experiences, our relationships, and in our "communities." God is the author of our life, the editor of our story, and our story must be one of surrender. God calls us to be servants to one another. In order to serve we must sacrifice and surrender our needs, on occasion. In asking you the reader to reflect on your journey and to examine your pathway to surrender, you should not proceed alone. Our Father knows we need His love and forgiveness {revealed through others} to sustain us as we journey the road of reconciliation and healing. With your "companion" and using the tools mentioned here in this chapter, become aware of the elements in your life, which you may need to surrender further; or, maybe you need to begin the surrendering process. And remember, this is a process, not an event!

Prayer of Abandonment
Brother Charles of Jesus

Father, I abandon myself into your hands.
Do with me what you will.
Whatever you may do, I thank you.
I am ready for all, I accept all.
Let only your will be done in me,
And in all your creatures.
I wish no more than this, O Lord.

Into your hands, I commend my soul;
I offer it to you with all the love of my heart,
For I love you, Lord, and so need to give myself
To surrender myself into your hands,

Without reserve and with boundless
confidence for you are my Father.

Chapter 10

Struggle

Some years ago a woman I'll call Judy came to me seeking spiritual direction. She did her "assignments" well—so well, in fact, that to me she seemed to be almost the perfect directee. At some point it became apparent, however, that Judy was completely out of touch with her real self and instead was hiding behind a perfect self that she was trying to create and maintain. Judy couldn't allow her true self to be seen because it was too painful and shameful. This became clear as we stood face-to-face with the heart of the conversion process, the most important part of the journey, a reconciliation between the ideal, her better self, and the real, herself as she really was.

This process of bringing together the ideal and the real is an ongoing part of our journey here on earth, and a spiritual director can help us with that. Perfectionism becomes our way to deny our wounds, which make up the fragmented self. The process of recognizing our unreal, or ideal, self and allowing our real self to be revealed is so important that until we enter it, very little growth, if any, can happen because we are dealing with what is unreal.

I invite you to think about and pray about what your ideal self might be like, and then describe it in writing. If you were able to realize all your dreams, all the things you ever really wanted without any opposition, without any struggle, what would that portrait of you look like? The more honest you are, the more the portrait will reflect your real values and priorities. You will likewise choose the things that help you to realize these very values because you are your values. It may be helpful to go back to the chapter on gifts and include in your self-portrait not only your gifts but also your weaknesses, areas where you need to grow. That is where all of us have the most difficulty.

There will always be tension in our lives between the ideal and the real. We might fall into the danger of searching for a life without tension. But that would be useless; struggle is the condition of our journey on this earth. As long as we are here, the struggle, the tension, between the ideal and the real goes on. But tension is good and growth producing if it is kept to a point that we can cope with it. Obviously, too much tension can kill us; if it doesn't kill our bodies, it can kill our souls. This is the difference between stress and distress. Stress, within limits, is good, but too much stress becomes distress.

Denying Our Brokenness

As we enter the process of reconciling the ideal and the real in our lives, we find that the first obstacle, and perhaps the most difficult obstacle to overcome, is denial. We all tend to deny that we are not perfect, we are sinful, we are broken, and we can make mistakes. We like to think of ourselves as perfect, but this is only an illusion. Truth is quite another matter.

Many types of behaviors become evident in a person who is in denial about their brokenness. In fact, most of those behaviors fall into several categories. In the categories I've listed here, each letter of the word denial represents a behavior that is typical of people who are in denial.

D– **Defensive.** We try to excuse ourselves. ("I'm not late. My alarm didn't go off.")

E– **Emotional.** When confronted about our

mistakes or shortcomings we get upset and
depressed. We tend to feel guilty.

N– **Negative.** We feel that we are no good. Our
self-esteem is nil.

I– **Immature.** We are irresponsible, doing nothing
to change or to grow in the areas where
change and growth are appropriate.

A– **Angry.** We are aggressive toward ourselves
and toward others. We are angry with the
world, but angrier, really, with ourselves.

L– **Lonely.** We feel that no one can help us. We
feel a painful sense of isolation.

To be in denial means to run away from the truth—
the truth of who we are, what we are, or where we are. God
loves us despite our sinfulness. He loves us just as we are.
If sinfulness stands in the way of our love for God, it is not
God's problem; it is our problem. So we need to identify the
areas where we are in denial, and then enter into the healing
process.

Forgiving Ourselves

Breaking through the denial of our own brokenness
requires forgiveness and reconciliation, and it begins when
we forgive ourselves. But forgiveness itself is a process.
How do we forgive ourselves? – By dying to our
self-centeredness. Dennis and Matthew Linn, in *Healing
Life's Hurts*[1], apply Elisabeth Kubler-Ross's five stages of
dying in *On Death and Dying*[2] to the process of forgiveness.
Here are the five stages, each followed by my comments:

1. **Denial** - This is the process in which we
    begin to recognize the illusions, the lies, the
    misconceptions of our lives, and admit that
    we are sinners, we are broken, and we need
    help. Although this is the first stage, it
    continues as we progress to the other stages.

2. **Anger** - When we begin to reflect on what we formerly denied about ourselves—how we've hurt ourselves and others by our failings—we may become angry. The truth may make us feel vulnerable, and anger is a natural defense mechanism. We use anger as a way of regaining a sense of power or protecting our vulnerability. But we must face our anger. We need to share our anger with a trustworthy person who can support us during this stage, so that we can break through our anger and move away from it.

3. **Bargaining** - Yes, I'll admit it if..." But really there are no ifs. We simply must realize that we have sinned and that God is loving and forgiving.

4. **Depression** - This is the stage in which we begin to accept the whole unpleasant or messy thing that we have been denying.

5. **Acceptance** - We say to God, "Do with me what you will. Heal me, O Lord, and only you can, and will, heal me."

When we consider healing, we consider reconciliation and forgiveness. These considerations, as well, may be a struggle, but we have Christ's unconditional love and forgiveness, which call us to practice unconditional love and forgiveness, especially toward ourselves. We do this when we offer to Christ our hurts, our weaknesses, and our sins, and ask him to heal and transform us.

Jesus the Healer comes to us in the Sacrament of Reconciliation, that moment when we can come before him just as we are—sinful and sorrowful—and pray, "Lord, heal me and I shall be healed." It is a moment of truth and growth. We bring ourselves to reconciliation, knowing, in faith, that in our sinfulness, our brokenness, our struggles, in those areas we are so afraid of, this is the exact place where we are going to find the peace of Jesus, the Father, and the life-giving Spirit in our lives. The graces of this wonderful meeting between Christ and ourselves through the ministry of the priest come to us when we are ready to receive Christ's healing love, his forgiveness, and the grace to amend our lives, walk in God's love, and do God's will in ways that we have not done before. It is essential that we see the Sacrament of Reconciliation in the context of lifelong healing, and for that reason we need to receive this sacrament regularly throughout our lives.

As we approach the Sacrament of Reconciliation, love and forgiveness go hand in hand. To truly love is to forgive; to forgive is to love. One leads to a deeper appreciation of the other. We cannot separate these two in our lives because we are called to love and forgive daily. When we enter the process of forgiveness and reconciliation, we enter the process of healing. Confronting our denial is a struggle, a process, a journey, not an event. The same is true of forgiveness. It is a journey for life. However, Christ has promised us his unconditional love throughout our journey.

In reconciling with others, we must also come to forgiveness of our self, and we may find that forgiving ourselves is more of a challenge for us than forgiving others. As the veil of denial is lifted, the ideal self, the illusion of our perfection, begins to crumble. When we confront the more realistic and truthful reality of our self, we may at first experience self-disappointment, self-directed anger, and the "shadow side" of our shame, which punish us relentlessly. What sustains us through this process is the love and acceptance of others who are also on the journey of reconciliation.

Reconciling the ideal self with the real self is a

difficult process. Dying to the ideal self, the false illusions that have protected us, is distressing. This is a journey to the Cross where we sacrifice the ideal self for the truth, for rebirth, and for the resurrection of the true self. To accomplish this journey we need a supportive community of friends along the way.

Becoming reconciled to our real self includes recognizing our gifts and our weaknesses. Our gifts are given to us by God to be used for his glory and for the service of others, as well as for taking care of our own needs. Our weaknesses show us the areas where we need to grow. This growth is a result of the power of God's grace and of our own struggles. The process of growth is not an easy one; we need courage and strength to confront our fears so that we die to the self. In spiritual direction, the person seeking direction is challenged to become aware of their gifts and their limitations. A truthful assessment of oneself can be a fearful process. We fear disappointment, rejection, and abandonment. But an accurate sense of oneself leads to more accurate judgments and decisions about our life.

Facing Life's Challenges

Spirituality is reality. Our personal life experiences, and our awareness of and understanding of such experiences, including how our gifts and our weaknesses have developed through those experiences, provide each of us with a unique reality. To understand our life's journey and purpose is to understand the way God is uniquely relating to us, gifting us, and creating our living story with him. Thus, to live in reality, which is the spiritual truth of our existence, we must become aware of our reality. The more we are aware of our reality and the more we live in that reality, moment by moment, the more spiritually balanced our world is. If we are to move toward greater wholeness—that is, to grow spiritually, becoming who God has ordained us to be—we must live in our reality as truthfully as we can.

The following self-evaluation tool lists some of life's challenges. Each of the twenty items consists of two statements, representing the opposite extremes on a continuum from 1 to 10. The statement on the left is represented by the 1 on the continuum, and the statement on the right is represented by the 10. For each pair of statements, circle the number that describes your current experience. For example, if the statement on the left is not at all true for you but you don't fully identify with the statment on the right, your number on that continuum is probably between 6 and 9.

I try to avoid authority figures because I fear they will criticize me or judge me.	I am comfortable engaging in dialogue with authority figures, and feel secure in my own position.
1 2 3 4 5	6 7 8 9 10
The approval of others is very important to me, and I try to change myself to feel more liked and accepted.	I am happy with who I am, and I accept my best efforts as worthy even if others disapprove of me.
1 2 3 4 5	6 7 8 9 10
I have a keen eye for what changes people need to make in their lives, and I try to help them improve.	I accept others as they are, and I work with them amiably even when I disagree with them.
1 2 3 4 5	6 7 8 9 10

I feel frightened, defensive, or worthless when I am criticized.	I am open to constructive criticism and welcome it as a tool for growth.
1　2　3　4　5　6　7　8　9　1 0	
Almost nothing is too inconvenient or too costly to me if it helps someone else.	I am available to those in need within the reasonable limitations imposed by my own personal needs for adequate rest, nourishment, prayer, and family or vocational commitments.
1　2　3　4　5　6　7　8　9　1 0	
I have an overdeveloped sense of responsibility, and it is easier for me to be concerned with others than with myself. I feel that I must help make things the best they can be.	I accept the limitations of my own capabilities, can relinquish control of a situation to others even when I feel I could do a better job, and recognize the things that are God's work, not mine.
1　2　3　4　5　6　7　8　9　1 0	
I feel guilty about expressing my own desires, ideas, or needs, and usually give in to others.	I can agreeably disagree without being egotistical.
1　2　3　4　5　6　7　8　9　1 0	
I find myself attracted to emotionally unavailable people, and I work very hard to win their affection.	I try to surround myself with warm, nurturing people, and I give and receive affirmation.
1　2　3　4　5　6　7　8　9　1 0	

Deep down, I am afraid of being rejected or abandoned by someone I love and will do almost anything to hold on to a relationship; I am deeply loyal.	I can be and let be. I can let go when a relationship is not mutually supportive.
1 2 3 4 5 6 7 8 9 10	
I blame myself when things go wrong or when a relationship ends.	I accept my share of responsibility for my actions and can also readily identify the things I cannot control.
1 2 3 4 5 6 7 8 9 10	
I like to be surrounded by music, TV, noise, people, or excitement.	I need and crave a certain amount of solitude, quiet, and reflection.
1 2 3 4 5 6 7 8 9 10	
I really don't like myself very much and don't feel I deserve to be happy.	I feel that I am special and unique and that I was created for love and joy.
1 2 3 4 5 6 7 8 9 10	
I tend to brag about myself, magnifying my successes and pointing out my accomplishments. I crave recognition.	I know my strengths. My life will speak for itself. What others think doesn't change who I am.
1 2 3 4 5 6 7 8 9 10	
I like to be in charge. I like to have control over what happens to me. It is important to me to be helpful.	I can let go and take each situation as it comes.
1 2 3 4 5 6 7 8 9 10	

In my relationships I am much more in touch with my dream of how it could be than I am with the reality.	I am loving in good times and bad times. I love others as they are, and I expect the same from them.
1 2 3 4 5 6 7 8 9 1 0	
I try to appear happy when I am angry, sad, or afraid.	I acknowledge my true feelings to myself and express them to others in appropriate ways.
1 2 3 4 5 6 7 8 9 1 0	
It takes an earthquake to get me moving. I finally respond and produce under pressure.	I am proactive and self-motivated.
1 2 3 4 5 6 7 8 9 1 0	
I don't expect anyone to do something I wouldn't do myself. However, my demands are high, and I judge others and myself by strict standards.	I am gentle and affirming in my judgment of both others and myself.
1 2 3 4 5 6 7 8 9 1 0	
I am attracted to people I feel sorry for and can rescue.	I appropriately express my compassion for those who are needy, and allow myself to be cared for by others.
1 2 3 4 5 6 7 8 9 1 0	

I ignore my own needs and abdicate my responsibility to care for myself. I don't like to look at my own limitations.	I accept myself as a person with both gifts and limitations or weaknesses. I share my gifts, respect my limitations, and find appropriate ways to meet my needs.

1   2   3   4   5   6   7   8   9   1 0

As you reflect on your responses to the preceding questions, keep in mind that self-knowledge is the beginning of spiritual growth. The Life's Challenges tool can help us see some areas in our lives where we are struggling and where we need to grow. As we grow in these areas, we also grow spiritually.

Becoming More Aware

Another helpful tool for self-examination has been given to us by St. Ignatius of Loyola, through what he called the Examen of Consciousness. St. Ignatius believed that this process was important enough to be an essential part of our daily prayers. Through the regular examination of our consciousness—thanking God his for good gifts received that day, and asking the Holy Spirit to show us where in our day we felt drawn toward God and where in our day we turned away from God—we become more aware of how God sees our life and how God is working in our life. We can use the Examen of Consciousness to help us look at each area of our day to see where we have excelled and where we have failed. We can then bring ourselves as we are, and where we are, before God to receive his healing, life-giving grace.

This process also helps us examine our daily actions and attitudes, chart our intended course, and ask God to provide us with the resources and desire to carry out his will. Self-growth is God's will for us; it is part of our journey. Through self-examination as part of our regular prayer, we can discover our true selves and grow into the person God intended us to be. This state of humanness is not easy to obtain, nor maintain, but God has freely offered his forgiveness and companionship, through Christ and the Holy Spirit, to support us each step of the way.

Throughout our lives we are called to respond to God's love by truly loving the giftedness he bestowed on each of us as he created us in his image and likeness, and by loving those significant others who walk the journey with us. The gift of the Sacrament of Reconciliation grants us the grace to grow beyond our brokenness and to develop our God-given gifts. That grace builds into our lives an all-important accountability that is essential to our relationship to God, to ourselves, and to others. When we forget that accountability, we set ourselves back in our efforts to draw closer to God.

Truly loving God means that we love God, ourselves, and others in an ever deepening way throughout our lives. We are called to love as Jesus loved. The more we permit ourselves to love God, others and ourselves, the more we become like Christ. However, the more we love, the more we open our hearts to suffering. Jesus on the cross, with his arms open wide, loved humanity to the point of death. Through this perfect act of love, in this broken state (crying out in agony), Jesus gave humanity the greatest gift of all: love. We are called, like Christ, to open our hearts to love, to sacrifice, and to suffer. As we do this, we come to learn what true love is.

The Sacrament of Reconciliation fosters an abiding awareness of, and sorrow for, our sins—the virtue of "compunction of heart" talked about in Christian spirituality. We then become converted. Our self-centeredness is converted into a perfect act of our love—love that forgives us and releases us into the Father's arms. "Father, forgive them for they know what they do" (Luke 23:34). The suffering and sacrifice of God's only Son was borne out of relationship. God reached out to humanity through the most intimate part of himself, Jesus, to reestablish relationship with his people. Through his love we could be restored to righteousness. And we are called to join him in this process of restoring. The more we open ourselves to loving others, the more we become like Jesus on the cross, and the more we can cry out with him in his perfect act of love for the Father and for us, the great gift of forgiveness.

When Jesus hung on the cross he had to be angry because anger is the normal human response to hurt. He could have used that anger and that struggle, either positively or negatively. He could have destroyed those who hurt him—that is, all of us. But instead, he used his anger positively, and from his sacred lips came those words that form a perfect model for us in our own life's journey as we further develop each of our relationships.

Through reconciliation we can forgive, again and again, or as Jesus tells us, forgive seventy times seven. That is the new life the sacrament brings us. To forgive ourselves is the greatest struggle of all—to accept God's gift, to receive it, and to give it to each other because we have been forgiven ourselves in the pure grace of this sacrament, this special gift given to us by a merciful Father, and by Jesus, our brother and healer, and by the power of the Spirit ever present in our journey.

The task of a spiritual director, the person who walks the journey with us, reaches its high point, its most effective function, when we become aware of our sinfulness, our brokenness, and we struggle to move beyond denial. No one can do this alone. We need someone to listen in a sensitive way to our journey and to have a sense of where we came from, where we hope to go, and where we are at the present moment. This relationship is constantly being defined by the director and the directee so as to guard the sacredness of the individual soul being directed, to ensure the person's full freedom to face the issues that need to be faced.

To the degree that we are living reconciliation, we become evangelizers. We are transparent and the Good News of Jesus, our Reconciliation, touches those around us in a healing, life-giving way.

Key Ideas: To..."Struggle is the condition of our journey on this earth." We live in a constant state of tension between the "real" and true self created by God, and the "ideal" or false self manufactured by our fears of rejection, abandonment, and shame. Becoming more aware of this on going reality of struggle, growing in our self-knowledge, is the beginning of spiritual growth. Our ideal self keeps us in the dark, in denial, losing who we are and what we our in God. Our manufactured self may protect us from that which we fear the most, aloneness. Consequently, we lose the reality of our existence, and the grace poured out by God that is intended to move us closer to Him. Take some time to identify what your ideal self looks like. What areas of your true self are you in denial of? How does your ideal self conceal who you really are; in your relationships with others, with yourself, and with God? In order to find the answers to these questions you will likely have to seek out a trustworthy companion.

1. Dennis Linn and Matthew Linn, *Healing Life's Hurts: Healing Memories Through the Five Stages of Forgiveness* (New York: Paulist Press, 1978).

2. Elisabeth Kubler-Ross *On Death and Dying* (New York: Macmillan, 1969), as cited in Linn, 9.

Balance

In seeking spiritual direction, it helps to begin by asking, "What are my greatest fears and my expectations about myself in my daily life?" I have a list of concerns that people often have when they come for a retreat or to look for a spiritual director. I call these concerns common reality and have listed them here in terms of questions:

- Where do I go from here?
- Do I understand and am I comfortable with my sexual feelings?
- Although I am hurting, am I able to touch others in a healing way?
- Family and friends have been so supportive, but can I accept their help?
- How can I avoid the extremes? Where do I find balance? Where do I find help in this struggle?
- I fear that my prayer life will be lost in the rush of each day. Will I give attention and time to reflection and prayer?
- Where should I look for support? Should I try to do it all by myself?
- Does anybody really care?

These questions reflect the common concerns that we all experience and have to confront nearly every day.

Those who are seeking spiritual direction are seeking guidance, reassurance, support, and encouragement. Most of us need affirmation and confirmation along the journey. And those who are in spiritual direction are no different; they simply are aware of their concerns and are choosing to receive spiritual direction as one way of seeking God's perspective on those concerns.

The common realities that we share as human beings reflect our life's circumstances and the cross we bear. The realities of work, family, and prayer impact us and challenge us to be transformed so that become more like Christ. These challenges can affect our sense of balance; they can cause distraction, conflict, blocks to our progress. Establishing or restoring the balance in our daily life is

critical in order for us to become free enough to hear and understand how God is speaking to us personally.

As we try to achieve balance in our lives, we have three categories of realities to deal with daily: prayer, family, and work or ministry. We might put it another way: our personal needs, the needs of our family or peer group, and the needs that must be met in the work that we do day after day. It is not just one or two of these that we must deal with each day; it is all three. They have a priority that makes it possible to do all three and to keep them balanced in our daily lives.

The first, and the most important of the three, is prayer. This includes prayer for our own personal needs, particularly at the beginning of the day. We all need to be with the Lord and to realize that this day is a day in which we are called to reach out as well as we can and do whatever God asks of us. We can then reach out to those nearest and dearest to us—our family, our community, our peers who work with us. We must be aware of their needs for our time and our energy. From there, we go out into the world around us, the world in which we live and move and work each day, and we try to meet the many demands that are made on us.

It is important to keep these three realities in their proper order: prayer, then family, and then work or ministry. If we turn these upside down, we might say, "First, there is my work. If I have time, I will be with my family or community, and if I have time left over after that, I'll spend some time in prayer. But if we do that, our lives go out of balance. These three things are intimately related, and we must keep them in their proper order.

One way we can keep balance in our lives is to learn how to say yes and no. We have heard of great mortifications, of wearing a hair shirt or a pebble in your shoe or of afflicting physical sufferings upon yourself as a way to achieve sanctity. However, I would offer that the greatest mortification any one of us can do is to develop that ability, at any given time or place, to say yes or no—whichever is appropriate to the situation.

We often believe that we can somehow live without taking care of ourselves. We were, likewise, given the idea that we are called to be a "yes" person, which is a distorted idea when it means unreflectively helping, or attempting to help, others. A "yes" person says yes to all requests, invitations, and suggestions in work, family, church, and elsewhere, and becomes overextended, even in their search for "holiness." A "yes" person seeks to please everyone and may feel the need to sacrifice their own needs for everyone else. It's a kind of martyr syndrome. In reality, the "yes" person fails to establish clear and healthy boundaries in their life, boundaries that would help them create the essential balance in their lives. The "yes" person has poor interpersonal boundaries, often failing to take care of themselves, often burning out, feeling empty, and sometimes becoming embittered because of not finding fulfillment of their own needs. God wants us to be charitable, generous, and giving of ourselves, but we also need to receive from others. Learning to say yes and no, when it is appropriate, is critical to our life's balance. Saying yes and no when we mean it can provide a balance in our life that frees us to serve others in ways that God intended.

We can help others only to the extent that we have taken care of our own needs. So we need to keep the proper order in the pyramid. If we do, we will become fruitful in all three of those basic areas.

To do this, we must begin by looking at the first level, prayer for our own personal needs. When we don't take care of our own needs we burn out. It has been my experience in working with persons who experience burnout, that burnout happens when we get the pyramid in the wrong order and expect to give beyond what we are able to give. One day we get up to start a new day, only to find that our vision, our energy—everything—is gone, and we fall apart. If we are to keep the pyramid in its proper order, we must make prayer for our own needs the foundation of our lives.

I find that the three elements of the pyramid actually reflect five basic realities of our daily life: the realities of sleeping, eating, playing, praying, and working. A problem develops when we take any one of these five realities and either overdo them or neglect them. For example, suppose we spend all our time in prayer, skip our meals, and do not take time for leisure, believing that if we would just spend more time praying, nothing would go wrong. Well, nothing will go wrong except that we are neglecting our own needs. We find ourselves getting out of proportion, and therefore the other areas go off balance.

Sometimes we forget that our work is really God's work. God gave us talents so that we might carry out his work, not our own, in his way. It is important that we pray to keep things in perspective. We also need to work, but we need to keep work in balance. Workaholism is the curse of our time. We can get so involved in our work, not just physically being at the office or our place of employment, but all day and all night long so that we never stop thinking about our work. Our work can take every bit of our attention, every bit of our energy, both physical and emotional. A person who has work out of balance tends to develop a messiah complex. If I'm not there, what will happen? The answer to that, of course, is that it will go very well—the way God wants it to go. God doesn't need us to do his work. He chooses us sometimes to do it. Therefore, he wants us to work within our own capabilities of time and energy. So when we pray, we pray; when we work, we work.

It is also important that we eat properly. We live in a country of extremes. Most of us are either dieting or eating too much. Eating a meal is not just for the purpose of nourishing ourselves. It is intended also as a time of relaxation. We sit down to have some time together and to have a meal. When the meal is over, we can get up feeling relaxed and go on with our work. If we do not sit down and relax when we eat a meal, we tend to overeat and can easily develop a weight problem. Conversely, if we don't take enough time to eat, we end up with other health problems. All these are problems that come from living an unbalanced life, of putting impossible expectations on ourselves because we have not sat down to think about them. Pray. Work. Eat. Sleep. Play.

Sleep is something without which we can't survive. Too much sleep can be an escape from reality; too little can inhibit our ability to work and pray and take care of our other needs. If we work all day and come in at night and watch the late, late show, and then go to bed late when we have to get up early the next morning, we find that our work is affected. We can't do that consistently, or else we become tired, lacking energy and finding that we can't concentrate on our work. Pray. Work. Eat. Sleep. Play.

Leisure, next to prayer, is probably the most difficult task for us to find time. We have set many goals for ourselves. We try to nourish many other people and take care of their needs, but it's difficult for us to find time each day to sit down and nourish ourselves. Do we ever ask ourselves, "Now, what do I need to do that I enjoy doing?" Leisure means doing what we enjoy doing, what nurtures us emotionally. It might be sports. It might be walking. It might be listening to music, or playing a musical instrument. It might be reading a book. But it must be something that nourishes us.

We overcome the tendency to burn out by keeping prayer, work, eating, sleeping, and leisure in balance. We keep them in balance by paying attention to them every day. In doing so, we not only establish a structure for our day, but we also give ourselves an internal sense of balance, accomplishment, and fulfillment.

The balance that I'm talking about is something that a spiritual director can help us develop. If you wrote down your daily schedule for any given 24-hour period, are these five things included? You could then work out for yourself an ideal schedule, try to follow it, and build some accountability into your life. If we live our lives without any accountability, it is easy to get off the track and lose the balance. While we can care for everyone else, we may sometimes feel, "No one cares for me." Sometimes we need to ask for help, and a spiritual director can give us that help. We create a program, and we sit down and talk with our spiritual director about our time management. I have yet to find anyone who does not mean well and starts out well. But when it comes down to working into a healthy daily pattern, we can do it only with the help of a spiritual companion or a spiritual director, who can help us be accountable, face our life as it evolves each day, and make adjustments until we fine-tune our original vision.

Eventually, with the help of prayer and a consistent pattern and the accountability of spiritual direction, you might develop what we call a leadership style. What is your style of leadership? I'd like to discuss several principles of leadership that can help you develop a balanced routine of attending to your own needs, the needs of those around you, and the needs of those you are called to serve. One purpose of leadership is, as Jesus tells us in the Gospel, to focus our work on the needs of others. Often, especially when we have done extensive academic preparation for the work we plan to do, we have an exact idea of the way it should be done, and we feel the need for our program to work. Sometimes we can be so taken up with this idea that we don't hear the needs of others. But we are there to serve them, to meet them in their needs by using our own gifts, talents, vision, and background.

Another purpose of leadership is to draw other people out, to help them do what they need to do, rather than do it for them. Often, people ask us to do things that they can do as well as we do, but they are used to letting someone else do it. Real leaders, in serving people's needs, see the giftedness of the those they're working with, and those leaders identify, encourage, and affirm that giftedness. In so doing, they help others to accomplish what they need to do.

A third purpose of leadership is to organize ourselves out of our work. Effective leaders do not set themselves above others and use others to meet their needs. Instead, effective leaders help others come to know and recognize their own needs, their own gifts, and ways they might meet their own needs. When that process is complete, the leaders are ready to move on to something else. We must remember that our involvement as leaders requires a certain detachment, so that we can let go at the appropriate time. This is the pattern of a life of service to which we are called. When we are unable to have that detachment for what we do, and we don't have our lives centered in God and in prayer, we can easily fall into the pit of obsession. We become obsessed about our work, and our relationships suffer. But if we have a healthy detachment, we can be truly thankful for our work as it is this day, for the challenges we receive each day, and for the ability that God has given us to be detached.

Often, leaders identify their work with themselves, so that when they leave, everything they've worked for collapses. But that is not leadership. Learning to lead effectively calls for a great deal of selflessness. We must set aside our human tendency to be egocentric. We must think of others rather than ourselves because the goal of all Christian ministry is to make Christ present to his people. We make Christ present to each other by our love and care, our kindness, our consideration, and our compassion toward others.

A fourth purpose of leadership is to be able to receive from those we serve. One of the hardest things to learn, next to saying yes or no, is to receive as well as to give—to be loved as well as to love. The people we serve need not only to receive our love, our concern, and our care, but also to show us how grateful they are. Expressing gratitude is a sign of a well-adjusted life. It is a wonderful thing when people tell us how we have helped them and they thank us for what we have done. When we can receive their gratitude graciously, we grow in our service to God and to each other.

I believe that these thoughts about keeping balance and developing a leadership style are some of the fruits we must pursue in spiritual direction. Two crises of our own age are spirituality and leadership. The crisis of spirituality is being addressed more and more each day with a myriad of books being written on this subject. The other crisis that is now coming into focus is leadership. But leadership that arises from a balanced life, and that is characterized by the purposes I have discussed, teaches others how to live the balanced, healthy life that God intends for them.

Key Ideas: Establishing balance in our daily life is critical. This allows us to become free enough to heed and respond to God's calling in our life. We are confronted daily by the realities of work, family, and our spirituality {prayer}. Our ability to set healthy boundaries, through our appropriate use of the words "yes" and "no," is essential. It allows us to create a place of silence, a place of sharing. Do you have difficulties saying "yes" and/or "no" appropriately? Where in your daily realities should you be saying "yes" and "no" more often, or less often? Do you have a leadership style? Where do you need the support of others to assist you in your efforts to focus on others needs, draw others out, and organize your responsibilities? God's reality is one of balance. All around us the world of nature speaks to this reality.

Vision

T he process of creating this book of reflections
on the art of spiritual direction has been
one of sharing and listening—sharing
the chapters with others, and listening to the
comments offered by these willing readers. The
one question that was asked repeatedly was,
"What was the main inspiration for the structure of these reflections?" In this chapter I'll try
to describe that vision.

The Rite of Christian Initiation for Adults (RCIA),
which is one of the great graces of the Vatican II Council,
impressed me and moved me to look at my own story, the
structures, people, and events that brought me to where I
am today. As I studied some of the first writings about the
RCIA and, in particular, an article published in Worship
magazine, I began to appreciate that after Vatican II we
have the structure for spiritual development in the Church,
in the faith community.

As we have learned in walking the journey through
spiritual direction, we find the answers to many of life's
questions in the reality of daily living. Answers to the
questions don't fall from heaven. They come to us because
we face the problems and work our way through them. We
have talked so much about the ideal and the real side of life.
This is the other side, the completion of the Paschal
Mystery, that we are called to confront each day of our
lives, to die to ourselves, to die to the past, to be alive in the

present and future, and to look forward to eternal life to which we are called through the Cross. This is reality. Are we going to continue to try to change the reality of God's will, or are we going to let it change and form us? In walking the way that Jesus pointed out to us, we need to accept his way, to deal with the wisdom of the Gospel, the Good News, in the reality in which we live.

The four steps of the RCIA framework are Inquiry, Catechumenate, Illumination, and Mystagogy. This forms the framework of our own journey. From these four pillars in the framework, we can talk about seven "Let there be,s"—seven indicators along the way of our journey that clearly point us toward the goal of the journey, our continual growth in our faith, our hope, and our love. Here are the seven:

Let there be storytelling. It is crucial for us to get in touch with our own unique personal story—to know who we are and how gifted we are. Telling our story helps us also to identify the challenges in our lives, learn to celebrate our values, and stay committed to our priorities day after day. This makes up our story.

Let there be questioning. As part of this Inquiry, we always look at our own lives because it is there, in our story, that we will find God's will for us. Each one of us is a unique creation of God, on a journey given to us by God, and blessed with gifts to carry out the will of God. Throughout our journey, there constantly must be questioning. Let us question and reflectively pray over our journey, our story, because therein we will find not only God's will for us but God's love and God's presence ever manifesting itself more clearly, more powerfully, so that we embrace the Gospel. Questioning is an invitation for us to reflect more deeply and to pray. If I find that I am not questioning, this is usually an indication that control is an issue for me. I arrange things the way I want them, only to find that God has different ideas.

Let there be communities of faith. Today we see an amazing increase of small faith communities within parishes. These are groups of people who want to share their faith in life-giving and receiving ways. The only way we can appreciate this is by doing it.

Let there be tradition. The Church Fathers and the many great saints who have gone before us showed us the way and gave us a background to see how the Gospel was lived uniquely in each of their lives. As we know, we are called to live that Gospel in our own lives and in our own times. We then come to realize that the more we walk the journey, the more we learn, the more we become acquainted, through the Catechumenate, with the nature of the community.

Let there be conversion. This is the Illumination, which is an ongoing process. This journey is a journey of growth into the fullness of the gifts God has given us. We are constantly going through conversions in our lives. We are being illuminated by the Light that is Christ and the Love of the Holy Spirit as we make our way back to the Father fully realizing the gifts that he has given us.

Let there be celebration. We celebrate by sharing in the sacraments—the Eucharist, Baptism, Confirmation. This continues the celebration of the love to which we are called in Christ Jesus, by letting Christ live in us and through us. We then can reach out to others in service.

Let there be ministries. This part of the framework, in which we serve others, is the fruit of all that we have experienced in our journey with Christ.

Now we have a structure for a lifelong program, a vision of what tomorrow, the next day, the next year, if God gives it to us, will be and will continue to be—an assurance on the road we are to walk.

As I experience this structure myself and help others to experience it, and as I grow in faith, I also grow in my love for God and others in my ability to forgive, to be kind, and to be compassionate. All these traits represent the deepest call that I hear in the core of my being—which God created and where God dwells. This is true in each of our lives. This is the window to the future. I rejoice in this vision that Vatican II has given. Now I can enter into this journey and not only have a guiding vision, but actually experience it at ever deeper levels. As I walk the journey, I move more deeply into my relationship with God and with others. I move more into the core of my being—to be who I am, where I am, and what I am. It is my prayer that you will experience this as well.

Let us thank God for who we are, what we are, and where we are—now, at this very moment—and find our stability, our continuity, in this deep belief. We are often tempted to look elsewhere. Yet, when we come to know who we are and where we are, we can thank God for putting us where we are and for making us who we are. Truly, we then can be ever more closely united to God and we can reflect God's love.

Key Ideas: We are all seeking answers to our basic daily questions, who am I, where am I, what am I. The answers to these simple yet profound questions are embedded in our daily realities of prayer, family, and work. These questions have been asked for generations and must continue to be asked. In engaging this process, we enter into the reality of life; moving ever closer to Our Father. What questions do you have regarding, who you are, where you are, what you are? Remember, the asking and the answering is not a singular event, but a life long journey. Our Father has promised to be with us every step of the way.

Directee's Comments

Comments About Father Luke from a Few of His Directees

"Father Luke was like a cool breeze on a hot summer day, a cold drink of water after hard work in the sun, and a warm soothing oil, poured out by God on the wounds of my soul. He was a wonderful listener. His presence communicated unconditional love, acceptance, and regard for who I was. He created a sacred space where my soul could be exposed. He was a priest at times, a friend at other times, a father always. Father Luke invited me to slow down and stop running away from myself. He was consistent, available, and committed to me. His words were encouraging and supportive, his actions truthful. He wouldn't lavish false praise on me; instead, he spoke to me with empathy and compassion without compromising the truth. Like a good coach, he motivated me to practice, exercise, and develop my faith skills, and he stood beside me, encouraging me and cheering for me as I took my steps in faith. In developing my trust in him as my "father" I consequently developed trust in my Father in heaven. I had always feared God in a dysfunctional manner, but Father Luke helped wash away those fears over time. While the healing process was at times long and painful, Father Luke became God's healing hand. I was left knowing a heavenly Father who was truly loving, understanding, patient, and accepting of me in my greatest state of weakness."

—Russ McCormack, Psy.D

"I always felt [that Father Luke] had time for me. He always looked directly at me while we talked. Then he would repeat back to me what I had just said to him, using his own words but reflecting mine—sometimes adding his own experience of a similar situation—so I could see more plainly the real issue I was facing. He helped me to see that it was OK to just be in God's presence, not necessarily to "say prayers" all the time. In this way I could learn to listen to the Holy Spirit. I can remember a time when I was dealing with a particularly troubling issue but could not seem to put it into words. I guess I had stuffed it so far down that it was difficult to bring it up. Father Luke pinpointed exactly what the matter was. In looking back, I am sure that it was the Holy Spirit putting that gift of knowledge in Father Luke—and thanks be to God, because it relieved me. Father Luke let me see the beauty in my life and how I was becoming in tune with God's will for me at the moment. He helped me to let go of some old scruples so I could be free to grow spiritually, recognize my God-given gifts, and use them for His glory."

—Madeleine Wright

"Father Luke was a simple, well educated, uncomplicated man. He had no aura. Just that kind and understanding face. Father Luke's great quality was giving me his total attention. He was always there for me and my family. I knew I could call him anytime. We didn't always talk about my problems. He was well versed and we could talk about world events, movies, music, and especially sports. He was a great Padres and Chargers fan. We used to pray for the Chargers. He was my friend. A friend that has known me for most of my life and a good priest who helped me over some rough spots in my life."

—F.B.I.

"Father Luke continually affirmed me and reminded me to keep focused on my goals. Celebrating the sacrament of penance with Father Luke was always memorable, as he emphasized God's continuous, abiding love and forgiveness.

Father Luke affirmed me by reminding me of my gifts and encouraging me to use them wisely, and he challenged me by encouraging me in making difficult choices and sticking with them. He also reminded me of my necessary limitations. He was my friend."

—Father James J. Clarke

"Father Luke affirmed and modeled God's unconditional love. When I was feeling very judgmental toward myself, I felt Luke's acceptance nonetheless, and hence, God's grace. I felt profound peace, mingled with relief and joy. He was always very good at identifying specific talents and abilities I might have overlooked or discounted in myself. He was so able to channel God's grace—affirming the best and loving us through the worst in ourselves."

—Larry Wampler, Ph.D.

"Father Luke stressed the importance of maintaining balance in my life between prayer, work, rest, study, and recreation with my family. While I often did not succeed in maintaining this balance very well, Father Luke was always affirming and loving nonetheless. He respected me (and everyone) as a child of God with unique gifts and talents. When I would tell him that I failed to take the time my body needed to get in the proper amount of R&R or sleep, he would always point out that every day was a new day. He was truly a friend who accepted me for who and what I was. He was never judgmental, always loving, and always human."

—Deacon Frank J. Mercardante

About the Author

Father Luke Dougherty, O.S.B. was a monk of the Prince of Peace Abbey in Oceanside, California.

Father Luke made his first profession in 1950 at Saint Meinrad Archabbey in Indiana. He was ordained at Saint Meinrad in 1955. In 1958, he was chosen to be one of the founding monks of Saint Charles Priory—now Prince of Peace Abbey in Oceanside.

The greater part of his monastic and priestly life was spent in the vocation and formation field. In the 1960s, he worked in the Woodside Priory School while he completed the requirements for his Master's Degree in History at the University of Santa Clara. At that time, he collaborated with Monsignor Peter Armstrong of San Francisco Archdiocese in forming the Search for Christian Maturity Program for youth.

For some twenty years, he served on the San Diego Diocesan Vocation Team. During this time, he did formative work in Pre-seminary, Seminary and Deaconate Programs. From it's beginning, he served in the Ministry to Priests Programs.

Father Luke worked with Co-dependency and Dysfunctional Family Retreats and Workshops as well as with the Twelve Step Spirituality Program.

He also conducted retreats for priests and religious men and women at the Abbey and elsewhere and spent much of his time involved in spiritual direction.

About Prince of Peace Abbey

Prince of Peace Abbey, the Benedictine community where Father Luke lived and served, is located in north San Diego County, California, on a hill overlooking the Pacific Ocean. The abbey church provides a panoramic view of the ocean from the pews and choir stalls. The monks' cells, or private living quarters, also provide a view of the ocean. Occasionally, the winter rains bring flash flooding to the river valley, submerging or washing out the abbey's bridge, so that the abbey sits isolated on a peaceful island until the water subsides.

The history of the abbey dates back to 1957, when Bishop Francis Buddy of San Diego approached the monks of St. Meinrad Archabbey in Indiana about beginning a foundation in his diocese. The small group of pioneering monks from St. Meinrad stayed in a private home in Riverside, California while they searched for property for the new foundation. In June 1958 God's providence steered them to Oceanside, California, with the help of a local real estate agent who owned a large piece of property—119 acres—overlooking the ocean and the city. Although the property included a small ranch house, the conditions were primitive and the monks were unsure at first that the property was the best place for them. They began to call it Rattlesnake Hill, because of the many rattlesnakes they discovered there. After prayer and negotiations with its owner, however, the property was purchased and the monks began their monastic lifestyle. Called St. Charles Priory at that time, it was formed under the wise supervision and direction of the first Prior, Father Rudolph Siedling, O.S.B. The monks needed an adequate place to live, and a chapel, so they hired Foster Rhodes Jackson, an architect, to draw the plans for their future home.

Although the original plan was to have a school for boys, it became clear that this was too far beyond their resources. So, instead, St. Charles Priory became a liturgical center with a retreat house. Once the retreat house was built and established, men interested in living a monastic life began to appear on the hill. The first vocation to the monastery was Dale Thomas Black, a young Californian. After he began his formation, the monks received into their community the first clerical monk, Richard Wright, who is now the Abbot of Prince of Peace Abbey. In the 1980s the monastery was elevated to the status of abbey, and the name was changed to Prince of Peace Abbey.

Even before the 1980s, plans were made to build a new church for the abbey, as the monks and laypeople who began to associate with the monastery outgrew the small chapel and the retreat house lobby, which substituted for the church at Sunday's liturgies. The plans also included new living quarters for the monks—a real cloister separated from the general public. As funds and donations began to grace our monastery, those plans became a reality. It seemed that once we finished one project, another project for further growth and buildings began. An administration building, a gate house, a new visitors' center, and new retreatant rooms were added. In the cloister the monks would have a new recreation center, a formation classroom building, and a chapter house.

In the late 1980s those plans were almost ruined. An arsonist set three fires to the hill, causing extensive damage and nearly taking the lives of two residing monks. If they had not been roused from sleep, they surely would have died in the blaze.

Through the years many men have joined our community. Some have left and others have stayed, adding to the ambience of the monastery. All these men have been gifted in a variety of talents and skills, and they all matured in the spiritual life under the wisdom and spirituality of its fifth-century founder, St. Benedict.

Prince of Peace Abbey remains a liturgical center and a beacon to today's world. Retreats, days of recollection, and counseling have been a major part of our apostolate, or mission. A secondary apostolate of the monastery, due to the efforts, toil, and sensitive heart of Brother Benno Garrity, has been that of aiding the poor and destitute. We have been a source of aid to the extremely poor in Mexico, especially in Tijuana, through the efforts of the Missionaries of Charity, Casa de Pobres, Mercy City, and Save the Children.

Father Luke, who was one of the pioneering founders of the Prince of Peace community, drew many individuals to the monastery—lay, religious, and priestly— through his gifts as a spiritual director and retreat master. We are happy to see his work being published, not only to honor this man and his work but also to introduce others to Benet Hill and the Prince of Peace Abbey. We welcome you to come and visit us.

—Father Prior Sharbel

Prince of Peace Abbey
650 Benet Hill Road
Oceanside, CA 92058 USA

Telephone: (760) 967-4200
Website: www.princeofpeaceabbey.org/
Email: princeabby@aol.com

Prince of Peace Abbey Church

Sanctuary

Retreat House

About RPI Publishing

We invite you to visit our internet website at www.rpipublishing.com

RPI Publishing, Inc. was founded on the belief that people on a spiritual journey need support from one another. It can't be done alone; we need the help of others. It is for this reason that we encourage you to find people who understand and can share with you the journey.

We strongly recommend that you contact the organizations listed in our Links section to help you in your search for information, support and understanding.

We at RPI Publishing, Inc. also believe strongly in the power of the Twelve Steps. They offer a process of guidance that helps identify our wounds and then suggests, with God's help, ways to move toward healing. We offer a variety of books to help readers through the process of their spiritual healing journey.

We offer General and Christian self-help books. These books include materials for adult children from dysfunctional homes and for adults with Attention Deficit Disorder.

RPI Publishing, Inc.
1725 Kresky Ave.
Centralia, WA 98531
1-800-873-8384